First World War
and Army of Occupation
War Diary
France, Belgium and Germany

1 DIVISION
Divisional Troops
26 Brigade Royal Field Artillery
1 August 1914 - 25 March 1917

WO95/1250/1

The Naval & Military Press Ltd
www.nmarchive.com
Published in association with The National Archives

Published by

The Naval & Military Press Ltd

Unit 10 Ridgewood Industrial Park,
Uckfield, East Sussex,
TN22 5QE England
Tel: +44 (0) 1825 749494

www.naval-military-press.com

www.nmarchive.com

This diary has been reprinted in facsimile from the original. Any imperfections are inevitably reproduced and the quality may fall short of modern type and cartographic standards.

© Crown Copyright
Images reproduced by permission of The National Archives, London, England, 2015.

Contents

Document type	Place/Title	Date From	Date To
Heading	WO95/1250/1		
Heading	1914-1917 1st Division Troops 1st Division Brigade R.F.A. Aug 1914-Mar 1917 To 1 Arms And Became Arms Field Artillery Bde		
Heading	1st Division 1st Division XXVI Brigade R.F.A. Aug-Dec 1914		
Map	Part Of The Aisne Valley		
Heading	1st Division War Diary XXVI Brigade R.F.A. August 1914		
War Diary	Aldershot	06/08/1914	11/08/1914
War Diary	Southampton	16/08/1914	16/08/1914
War Diary	Boulogne	17/08/1914	19/08/1914
War Diary	Le Nouvion	20/08/1914	20/08/1914
War Diary	Boue	22/08/1914	26/08/1914
War Diary	Fesmy	27/08/1914	28/08/1914
War Diary	St Gobain	29/08/1914	31/08/1914
Heading	1st Division War Diary XXVI Brigade R.F.A. September 1914		
War Diary	St Gobain	29/08/1914	31/08/1914
War Diary	Villers Cotterets	01/09/1914	10/09/1914
War Diary	Treville	10/09/1914	30/09/1914
Miscellaneous	To A.G. Base	10/11/1914	10/11/1914
Miscellaneous	Casualties 26th Bde. R.F.A.		
Map	Maps		
Map			
Heading	XXVI ? 1st Div. B.E.F. 1914 From Bde (Stealt Col) Cunlitte Owen R.F.A.		
Heading	1st Division War Diary XXVI Brigade R.F.A. 1914		
War Diary	Pilkem	22/10/1914	25/10/1914
War Diary	Zillebeke	26/10/1914	31/10/1914
Miscellaneous			
Heading	1st Division. War Diary XXVI Brigade R.F.A. November 1914		
War Diary		31/10/1914	31/10/1914
War Diary		01/11/1914	05/11/1914
War Diary	Pargnan	01/10/1914	16/10/1914
War Diary	Fere-En-Tardenois	16/10/1914	16/10/1914
War Diary	Haze Brouck	17/10/1914	21/10/1914
War Diary	Langemarke	21/10/1914	21/10/1914
War Diary	Pilkem	22/10/1914	30/11/1914
Heading	1st Division War Diary XXVI Brigade R.F.A. December 1914		
Heading	XXVI Brigade Ammunition Column. R.F.A. August 1914		
War Diary		01/08/1914	31/08/1914
War Diary	Aldershot N.C.	05/08/1914	15/08/1914
War Diary	South Hamp	16/08/1914	16/08/1914
War Diary	Boulogne	17/08/1914	19/08/1914
War Diary	Bone	20/08/1914	21/08/1914
War Diary	Cartignies	21/08/1914	21/08/1914

War Diary	Line Of March	22/08/1914	22/08/1914
War Diary	Grand Regn	23/08/1914	26/08/1914
War Diary	Pont-Au-Cambreics	27/08/1914	27/08/1914
War Diary	St Gobain	25/08/1914	29/08/1914
War Diary	Allemant	30/08/1914	31/08/1914
Heading	1st Division War Diary XXVI Brigade Ammunition Column R.F.A. September 1914		
War Diary	Allemant	30/08/1914	01/09/1914
War Diary	Meaux	02/09/1914	03/09/1914
War Diary	Coulommiers	04/09/1914	16/09/1914
War Diary	Jumigny	17/09/1914	19/09/1914
War Diary	Jumigny	30/09/1914	30/09/1914
War Diary	Jumigny	21/09/1914	24/09/1914
War Diary	Pargnan	25/09/1914	27/09/1914
Heading	1st Division War Diary XXVI Brigade Ammunition Column R.F.A. October 1914		
War Diary	Pargnan	01/10/1914	14/10/1914
War Diary	Loupeigne	15/10/1914	15/10/1914
War Diary	Fere-En-Tardenois	16/10/1914	16/10/1914
War Diary	Cassel	17/10/1914	17/10/1914
War Diary	Hazebrouk	18/10/1914	19/10/1914
War Diary	Poperinge	20/10/1914	20/10/1914
War Diary	Pickem	21/10/1914	25/10/1914
War Diary	Zillebeke	26/10/1914	26/10/1914
War Diary	1/2 Min Sqveldhoea	27/10/1914	31/10/1914
Heading	1st Division 26th Bde R.F.A. War Diary 117th Battery R.F.A. August 1914		
War Diary		04/08/1914	15/08/1914
War Diary	Aldershot	16/08/1914	21/08/1914
War Diary	Cartigny	22/08/1914	31/08/1914
Heading	1st Division 26th Bde R.F.A. 117th Battery R.F.A. September 1914		
War Diary		01/09/1914	26/09/1914
War Diary		14/10/1914	23/10/1914
War Diary	1st Division 26th Bde. R.F.A. War Diary 117th Battery R.F.A. October 1614		
War Diary		26/09/1914	05/11/1914
Heading	1st Division 26th Bde. R.F.A. War Diary 117th Battery R.F.A. November 1914		
Miscellaneous	117 Bde R.F.A. 1914	01/11/1914	05/11/1914
War Diary		05/11/1914	22/11/1914
Heading	1st Division 26th Brigade R.F.A. Jan. To Dec. 1915.		
Heading	1st Division 26th Brigade R.F.A. Vol. VI.		
War Diary		01/01/1915	31/01/1915
Heading	1st Division 26th Bde. R.F.A. Vol. VIII. 1-28.02.15		
War Diary	Givenchy	01/02/1915	28/02/1915
Heading	1st Division 26th Bde. R.F.A. Vol. VIII. 1-31.03.15		
War Diary	Lillers	01/03/1915	01/03/1915
War Diary	Le Touret	02/03/1915	23/03/1915
War Diary	Richebourg	24/03/1915	31/03/1915
Heading	1st Division 21st Division 26th Bde. R.F.A. Vol. IX. 1-30.04.15		
War Diary	Richebourg	01/04/1915	30/04/1915
Heading	1st Division 26th Bde. R.F.A. Vol. X. 1-31.05.15		
War Diary	Richebourg	01/05/1915	15/05/1915
War Diary	Vermelles	16/05/1915	31/05/1915

Heading	1st Division 26th Bde. R.F.A. Vol. XI. 1-30.06.15		
War Diary	Vermelles Cuinchy	01/06/1915	14/06/1915
War Diary	Cuinchy	15/06/1915	18/06/1915
War Diary	Annezin	19/06/1915	23/06/1915
War Diary	Ferfay	24/06/1915	28/06/1915
War Diary	Vermelles	29/06/1915	30/06/1915
Heading	1st Division 26th Bde. R.F.A. Vol. XII. 1-31.04.15		
War Diary	Vermelles	01/07/1915	31/07/1915
Heading	1st Division 26th Bde. R.F.A. Vol. XIII. August. 15		
War Diary	Vermelles	01/08/1915	31/08/1915
Heading	War Diary Headquarters, 26th Brigade, R.F.A. 1st Div. Sept. 1915		
War Diary	Vermelles	01/09/1915	30/09/1915
Miscellaneous	1st Divisional Artillery Group Time Table.		
Miscellaneous	Targets For Batteries As Under		
Heading	1st Division 26th Bde. R.F.A. Oct 15 Vol XV		
War Diary	Vermelles	01/10/1915	16/10/1915
War Diary	Lapugnoy	17/10/1915	18/10/1915
War Diary	Marle-Les. Mines	19/10/1915	19/10/1915
War Diary	Lieres	20/10/1915	31/10/1915
Heading	1st Division 26th Bde. R.F.A. Nov Vol XVI		
War Diary	Lieres	01/11/1915	13/11/1915
War Diary	Fosse 7	15/11/1915	30/11/1915
Heading	1st Div 26th Bde. R.F.A. Dec Vol XVII		
War Diary	Fosse 7	01/12/1915	10/12/1915
War Diary	Fosse 7 & Vermelles	11/12/1915	31/12/1915
Heading	1st Division H.Q. 26th Brigade R.F.A. Jan-Dec 1916		
Heading	1st Divisional Artillery. H.Q. 26th Brigade R.F.A. January 1916		
War Diary	Vermelles & Fosse 7	01/01/1916	31/01/1916
Heading	1st Divisional Artillery 26th Brigade R.F.A. February 1916		
War Diary	Auchel	01/02/1916	16/02/1916
War Diary	Les Brebis	17/02/1916	29/02/1916
Miscellaneous	Operation Order Left Group		
Miscellaneous	A Form Messages And Signals.		
Miscellaneous			
Heading	1st Divisional Artillery. H. Q, 26th Brigade R.F.A. March. 1916		
War Diary	Les Brebis	01/03/1916	31/03/1916
Heading	1st Divisional Artillery. H.Q. 26th Brigade, R.F.A. April 1916		
War Diary	Les Brebis	01/04/1916	30/04/1916
Heading	1st Divisional Artillery. H.Q. Brigade R.F.A. May 1916		
War Diary	Les Brebis	01/05/1916	31/05/1916
Heading	1st Divisional Artillery. H.Q. Brigade R.F.A. June 1916		
War Diary	Grenay R. 5 D 9 10	01/06/1916	15/06/1916
War Diary	Grenay	16/06/1916	30/06/1916
Heading	1st Div. War Diary H.Q. Brigade R.F.A. July 1916		
Heading	Confidential War Diary of 26th Brigade R.F.A. May 1916 Vol. 24		
War Diary	Grenay	01/07/1916	03/07/1916
War Diary	Lozinghem	04/07/1916	06/07/1916
War Diary	Navernas	07/07/1916	07/07/1916
War Diary	Molliens Au Bois	08/07/1916	12/07/1916
War Diary	Behencourt	12/07/1916	13/07/1916

War Diary	In Defied	14/07/1916	18/07/1916
War Diary	Bottom Wood	19/07/1916	31/08/1916
Heading	1st Divisional Artillery 6th Brigade Royal Field Artillery August 1916		
Heading	War Diary of 26th Brigade Royal Field Artillery 1st to 31st August 1916 Vol. 25		
War Diary	Bottom Wood Ref. Map Sheet. 57d S. E. D. 2. B. Square X. 29	01/08/1916	31/08/1916
Miscellaneous	Bottom Wood	04/08/1916	31/08/1916
Heading	1st Divisional H.Q. 26th Brigade Royal Field Artillery September 1916		
War Diary	Bottom Wood X 29a Sheet. 57d S.E. Edin 2 b	01/09/1916	05/09/1916
War Diary	Wagon Lines F. 8.a Sheet 62d Behencourt Map Ref. As Alove	06/09/1916	30/09/1916
Heading	1st Divisional Artillery. H.Q. 26th Brigade Royal Field Artillery October 1916		
War Diary	Behencourt Sheet 62d E D N C 19A	01/10/1916	31/10/1916
Heading	1st Divisional Artillery. H.Q. 26th Brigade Royal Field Artillery November 1916		
War Diary	Behencourt Ref. Sheet. 62d 1st Ediam 6.19a	01/11/1916	20/11/1916
War Diary	Bottom Wood Sheet 57 S W 1/20000	21/11/1916	24/11/1916
War Diary	S 15 C 6.2 Sheet 57c S.W 1/20.000	25/11/1916	30/11/1916
Heading	1st Divisional Artillery. H.Q. 26th Brigade R.F.A. December 1916		
War Diary	S 15 A 6.1 Near Bazentin Le Grand Tos Map Sheet 57 S.W. Edlm 2nd 20.000	01/12/1916	31/12/1916
War Diary		14/12/1916	22/12/1916
War Diary		02/12/1916	13/12/1916
Heading	1st Division Royal Artillery 26th Brigade Royal R.F.A. Jan. To Mar. 1917		
Heading	War Diary 26th Brigade Royal Field Artillery 1st Division. January 1917		
War Diary	S 15 C 6.1 Sheet 57c S.W Edin 2d	01/01/1917	01/01/1917
War Diary	Molliens Au Bois	14/01/1916	31/01/1916
War Diary		14/01/1916	14/01/1916
Heading	War Diary 26th. Brigade, Royal Field Artillery. 1st. Division February 1917		
War Diary	Villers Brettonneux	01/02/1917	09/02/1917
War Diary	M6d5 Map-Sheet 62c S. W. E D T 2 A	10/02/1917	26/02/1917
Heading	26th Brigade. Royal Field Artillery 1st Division March 1917		
War Diary	Ref Sheet 62 S W M 6 D 51/12	01/03/1917	05/03/1917
War Diary	Ref Lens ll 1/100.000 Villers-Bocaee Outrebois	06/03/1917	09/03/1917
War Diary	Ref Lens ll 1/100.000 Outrebois Fillievres	09/03/1917	10/03/1917
War Diary	Bergueneuse	11/03/1917	11/03/1917
War Diary	Houdain	12/03/1917	12/03/1917
War Diary	Estree	13/03/1917	19/03/1917
War Diary	Cauchie	20/03/1917	21/03/1917
War Diary	Ref 51cNE ED2.F7d	22/03/1917	22/03/1917
War Diary	Rolincourt 1 Bn Wieb S A 25 B 1/2 725	23/03/1917	25/03/1917
War Diary	Ref. 51 C N E 26/31 E D 2 F7d	26/03/1917	26/03/1917
War Diary	Rolincourt 1 Bn Wieb S A25	23/03/1917	25/03/1917

W095/12501

1914-1917
1ST DIVISION Troops

26th BRIGDE R.F.A.

AUG 1914-MAR 1917

TO 1 ARMY
AND BECAME ARMY FIELD ARTILLERY BDE

1ST DIVISION

XXVI BRIGADE R.F.A.

AUG - DEC 1914

{ 117th Battery R.F.A. }
{ Ammn Column }

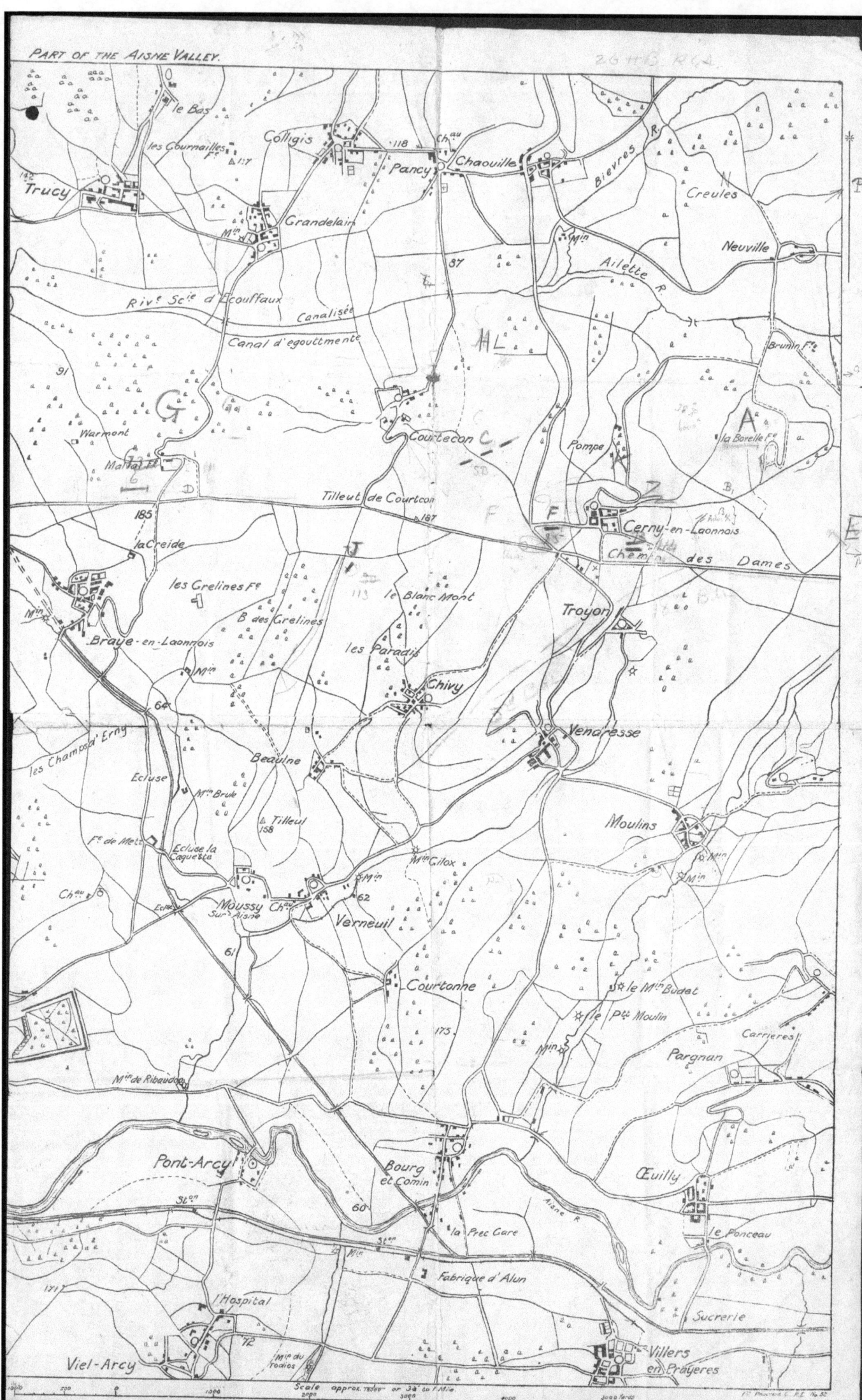

1st Dividon

WAR DIARY

XXVI BRIGADE   R. F. A.

August

1914

26th BRIGADE R.F.A.

WAR DIARY
or
INTELLIGENCE SUMMARY.
(Erase heading not required.)

Army Form C. 2118.

Hour, Date, Place	Summary of Events and Information	Remarks and references to Appendices
Aldershot 6.8.14	Mobilization commenced	First day, Sick day
" 11.8.14 5.30 p.m.	Mobilization completed	
Southampton 16.8.14	Embarked on S.S. Anglo-Canadian (No. 6 Bat. Amm. Column)	Sayoff Boulogne harbour from 5 a.m. – 5 p.m. 17.8.14. 116 Bty. embarked in 3 different ships – landed and complete to the Brigade. Arrived at R.v. dep 20.8.14. Reached 1307 in rest camp Rd. Justice 3 m. from Boulogne.
Boulogne 17.8.14 6 p.m.	Disembarked	
" — " 9 a.m.		
" 19.8.14 P.30 a.m.	Entrained (No. 11 & 116 Bty.) Travelled via Abbeville, Amiens, Busigny.	
Le Nouvion 20.8.14 5 a.m.	Detrained	
" — "	Marched to Boué. Billeted in 1st Brigade (Irish) Area	
Boué 22.8.14	— CARTIGNIES —	
" 23.8.14	— GRAND RENG —	
" 24.8.14	In action 3 m. S.E. of VILLERS-SIRE-NICOLE. No engagement	
" 8.30 p.m.	Marched to LA LONGUEVILLE	
25.8.14	— DOMPIERRE —	
26.8.14	— FESMY —	
FESMY 27.8.14 7 a.m.	Rearguard action. 1 Section 118 in action at 7 a.m. N of FESMY supporting Munsters further Rearguard of Brigade at Pont CARRIERES	
" 1.30 a.m.	Rearguard of 1st Bde & 25 Bde R.F.A. retired through ETREUX	
" 2.30 a.m.	2 Sections 118 supporting Black Watch on high ground N of ETREUX. E & W of FESMY – ETREUX road	
" 4 p.m.	118 in action N.W. of ETREUX – GUISE road. Coming retirement to Black Watch retired via ETREUX – GUISE road. Ike Section 118 B/2 out Munsters & in of reserve. Bivouaced at LA JUNQUIERE	

Army Form C. 2118.

WAR DIARY
or
INTELLIGENCE SUMMARY.
(Erase heading not required.)

Instructions regarding War Diaries and Intelligence Summaries are contained in F. S. Regs., Part II. and the Staff Manual respectively. Title pages will be prepared in manuscript.

Place	Date	Hour	Summary of Events and Information	Remarks and references to Appendices
	28/8/14		Marched to St GOBAIN with 1st Bde	
	29/8/14		Rest day	
	30/8/14		Marched to ALLEMANT	
	31/8/14		— VAUXBUIN	

1st Divison

WAR DIARY

XXVI BRIGADE R. F. A.

SEPTEMBER

1914

Attached: Casualties &
Shetch Maps

for Aug & Sept.

26th Brigade R.F.A

WAR DIARY
or
INTELLIGENCE SUMMARY.
(Erase heading not required.)

Army Form C. 2118

Hour, Date, Place	Summary of Events and Information	Remarks and references to Appendices
St GOBAIN 28.8.14	Marches to St GOBAIN with 1st Bde.	
29.8.14	Rest day.	
30.8.14	Marched to ALLEMANT	
31.8.14	— VAUXAIN	
VILLERS-COTTERETS 1.9.14 1.30 p.m.	116 F.Bty in action ½ mile S of VILLERS-COTTERETS with Bryans mortars covering retirement of 1st Bde from the town. No casualties. Bivouacked 1 mile S of LA FERTÉ-MILON.	
2.9.14	Marches to CHAMBRY	
3.9.14	— LA FERTÉ-SOUS-JOUARRE	
4.9.14	— COULOMMIERS & Bivouacked 1 mile S.	
5.9.14	— "NESLE"	
6.9.14 9 a.m.	116 F.Bty with Grenadiers finds an advanced guard to 15th Bde.	
9 a.m.	116 in action (out of action) with 4th Inniskillings.	
9.45 a.m.	117 in action near pt 109 W of 4th Inniskillings	
10.15 a.m.	118 at VRIGNEL FME	
5 p.m.	116 returns to position of readiness at MON PLAISIR	
7.9.14 6 a.m.	Bde advances to PUISEAU & bivouacs. Shells in wave by 2nd Division	
10.15 a.m.	26th Bde in action N of PUISEAU. No engagement.	
8.9.14 8 a.m.	Marches with 1st Bde to LA FRÉNOY near CHOISY	
11 a.m.	116 F.Bde as advanced guard shelled in road just S of BEZZOT	
	116 & 118 in action S of BEZZOT	

III

96th Brigade R.F.A

Army Form C. 2118

WAR DIARY
or
INTELLIGENCE SUMMARY.
(Erase heading not required.)

Instructions regarding War Diaries and Intelligence Summaries are contained in F.S. Regs., Part II. and the Staff Manual respectively. Title pages will be prepared in manuscript.

Place	Hour, Date	Summary of Events and Information	Remarks and references to Appendices
	8.9.14	March continued to bivouac N of HON DE VILLIERS	
	5 p.m.	116 moved out of bivouac & shelled column moving through NOGENT	
	9.9.14	Marches to LANOUETTE FME about 4 m N of SAULCHERY	
	10.9.14	Marched to COURCHAMPS	
	12.30 pm	In Rendezvous just N of COURCHAMPS	
		Advanced continued to LATILLY via SOMMERANS.	
TREVILLE	3.30 pm	116 in action at TREVILLE against Cuirass'rs at CHOUY	
	11.9.14	Marched with 1st Bde on Div'l Flank & to TRUGNY	
	12.9.14	Marches to BAZOCHES.	
	13.9.14	Marches to BOURG crossed river by Canal bridge	
	14.9.14 11 a.m.	116 with 1st Bde as advanced guard. 117 + 118 Marched to TOUR DE PAISY	
	8 a.m.	117 TFR in action at HARPE DE PAISY	
	10.30 a.m.	118 advanced to position just S of 110 in CHEMIN DES DAMES	
	15.9.14 4.30 a.m.	Both batteries engaged all day. 116 with 1st Bde near VENDRESSE	
		130 R batterie in same position. Enemy made an attack about 8 p.m. from	
		direction of N of CERNY which was repulsed	
	4 p.m.	117 heavily shelled by the heavy howitzers. Positions barely by aeroplane.	
		130 R batterie withdrawn at dusk.	
	16.9.14 4.30 a.m.	117 in same position entrenched. 117 entrenched about C of LFT CREUTES	
		Engaged with enemys artillery all day.	
	17.9.14 4.30 a.m.	Same positions. Enemy made such attack in evening driven back	
		TURCO battalion on our right. 118 withdrew to 300 N E of TOUR DE PAISY	

(9 29 6) W 3332—1107 100,000 10/18 H W V Forms/C. 2118/10.

26th Brigade R.F.A.

Army Form C. 2118

WAR DIARY
or
INTELLIGENCE SUMMARY.
(Erase heading not required.)

Instructions regarding War Diaries and Intelligence Summaries are contained in F.S. Regs., Part II. and the Staff Manual respectively. Title pages will be prepared in manuscript.

Hour, Date, Place	Summary of Events and Information	Remarks and references to Appendices
17.9.14. about 3p.m.	Enemy attacked from direction of CERNY Both Batteries shelling M. of CERNY	
18.9.14. 4.30 a.m.	Same position. Artillery engagements during day	
19.9.14. 4.30 a.m.	Same position " "	
20.9.14. 4.30 a.m.	Same position. Enemy made 2 attacks during the day. 117 shelled by tanks by aeroplane & shells by heavy hows. 2 guns disabled.	
21.9.14. 4.30 a.m.	117 moves to position to N. of TOUR DE PRISSY FME 118 in same position. Both Engaged with enemy. Anything about CERNY & PARGNERE.	
22.9.14. 4.30 a.m.	Same position. 118 shelled by heavy hows 300 all day. 1 gun disabled. Both engaged with enemy guns about CERNY & PARGNIER	
23.9.14. 4.30 a.m. 8.30 a.m.	118 moves 300 yards W. of last position. Both batteries opened fire on IMPROVISE TROOPS in support of Gen. Ct. attack on LA CREUTE & MORTERISE FME.	
24.9.14. 4.30 a.m.	Both Batteries in same position. Artillery engagement all day. Both batteries engaged enemy. Shelled by heavy howitzers.	
25.9.14. 3 a.m. 4.30 a.m. 4 p.m.	Relieved by 57st 13 Battery. Withdrawn to PARGNAN. 4 guns of 117 & 2 guns 118 in enclave cross the position 400 yards W of PARGNAN Shelled by heavy howitzers.	
26.9.14.	Same position. 2 damaged guns of 117 & 118 withdrawn from PRISSY ridge during night of 28/29	
27 – 30.9.14	Same position. No firing	

To A.G. Base

Herewith list of Casualties of Brigade under my Command from 16.8.14 – 30.9.14. which should have been entered in the War Diary for that period

C. Cunliffe Owen Col Cmdg
26th Bde R.F.A.

10.11.14

Casualties 26th Bde R.F.A. 16.8.14 — 30.9.14.

	HQr.	116	117	118	A.C.
26.8.14	1 m.				
27.8.14			2 w.	2 w. Major Bayley ⎫ Lt Stewart Cox⎬ missing 40 OR ⎭	
3.9.14			2 w.		
6.9.14			1 w.		
8.9.14	Capt Scatchard R.A.M.C. ⎫ 2 OR ⎬ k 3 OR. w.				
14		Maj. Nicholson ⎫ w. 4 OR ⎭			
15		Lt Swinton . k 2 OR. w.	Lt Hayes ⎫ w 6 OR ⎭ 3 OR . k.	1 OR. k.	
17			1. w.		
18		1 m.			
19			Maj. Rehard w.		
20			2/Lt Balfour ⎫ w 8. OR ⎭		
22		1 w.		4 w.	

Casualties 26th Bde R.F.A

	116	117	118	Q.C.
23.9.14		1 K / 4 W	1 W	
24		1 K	1 K	
25			1 K / 2 W	
26	1 W			1 W
27	1 K			
29	1 W			

C. Crubyffe Order Col Cmrg
26th Bde R.F.A.

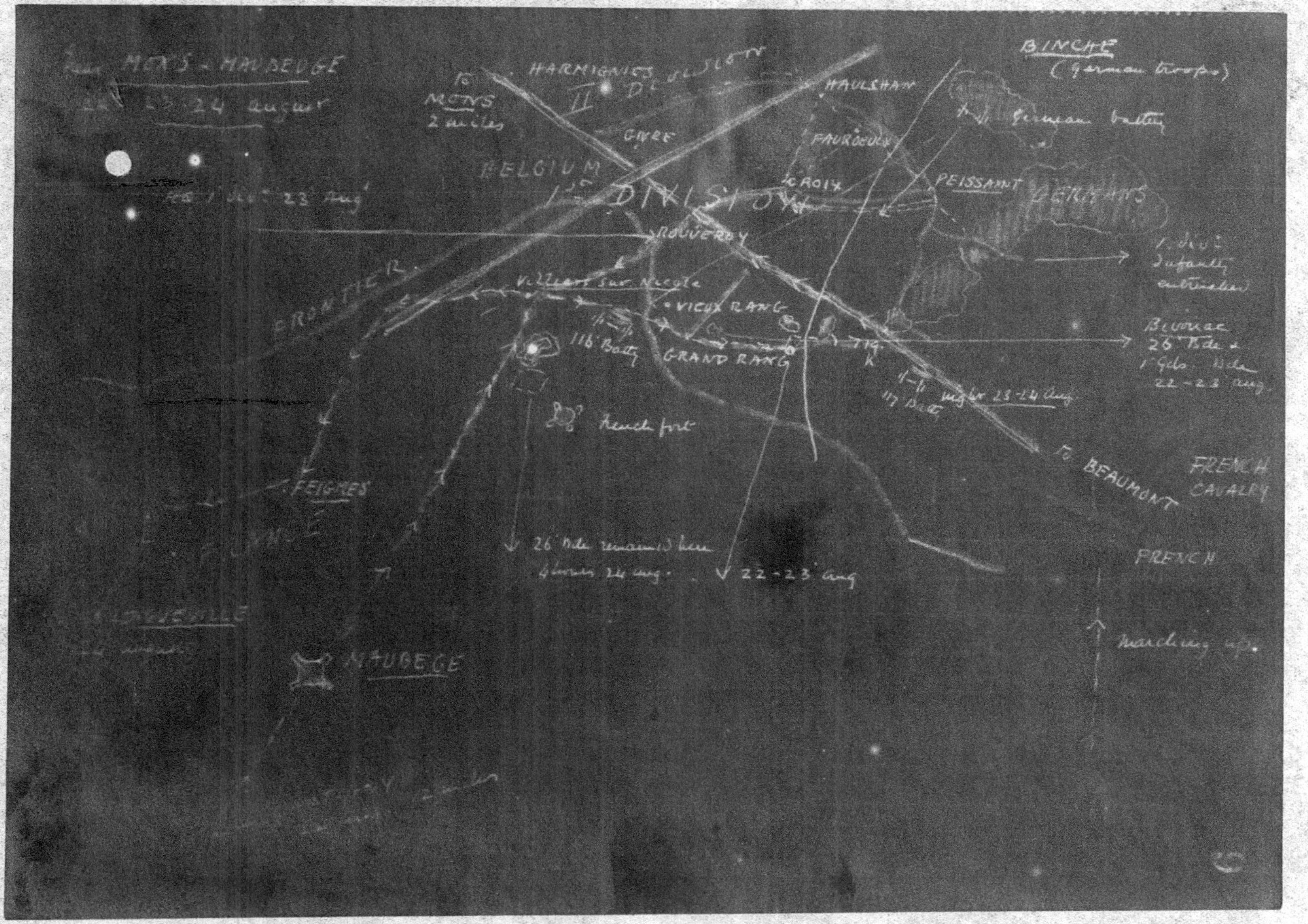

MONS – MAUBEUGE
23–24 August
HARMIGNIES
II DIVISION
To MONS 2 miles
GIVRY
BELGIUM
1st DIVISION
HAULCHIN
FAUROEULX
CROIX
PEISSANT
GERMANS
BINCHE (German troops)
German battery
ROUVEROY
FRONTIER
Villers sur Nicole
VIEUX RANG
GRAND RANG
116 Batty
117 Batty
night 23–24 Aug
French fort
FEIGNIES
26 Bde remained here
22–23 Aug
Bivouac 26 Bde 22–23 Aug.
To BEAUMONT
FRENCH CAVALRY
FRENCH
marching up.
MAUBEGE

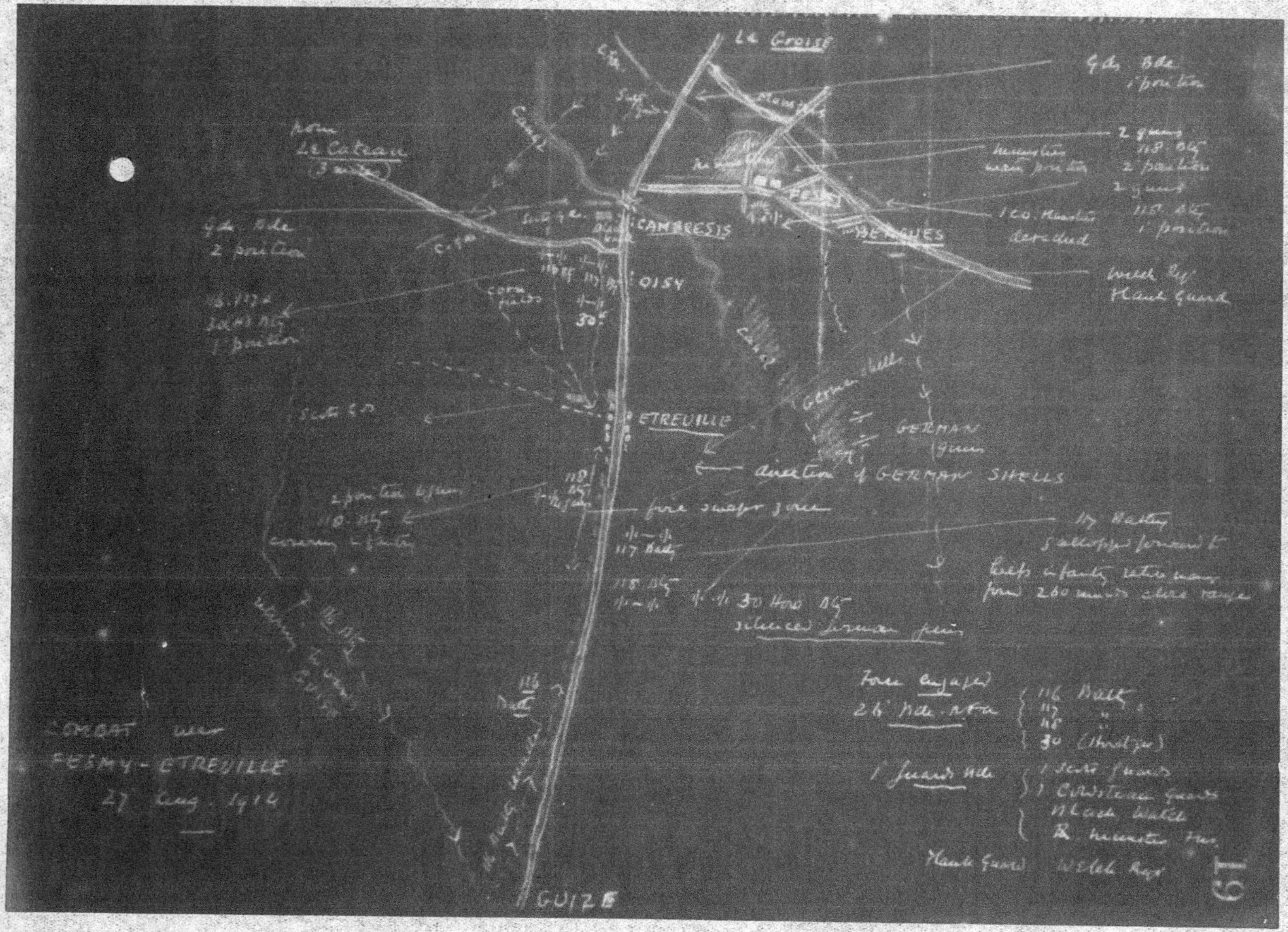
LE GROISE
LE CATEAU
CAMBRESIS
OISY
ETREUILLE
GERMAN
direction of GERMAN SHELLS
GUIZE
COMBAT near
FESMY - ETREUILLE
27 Aug. 1914
Force engaged
26 Bde. R.F.A.
1 Guards Bde
Welch Regt
19

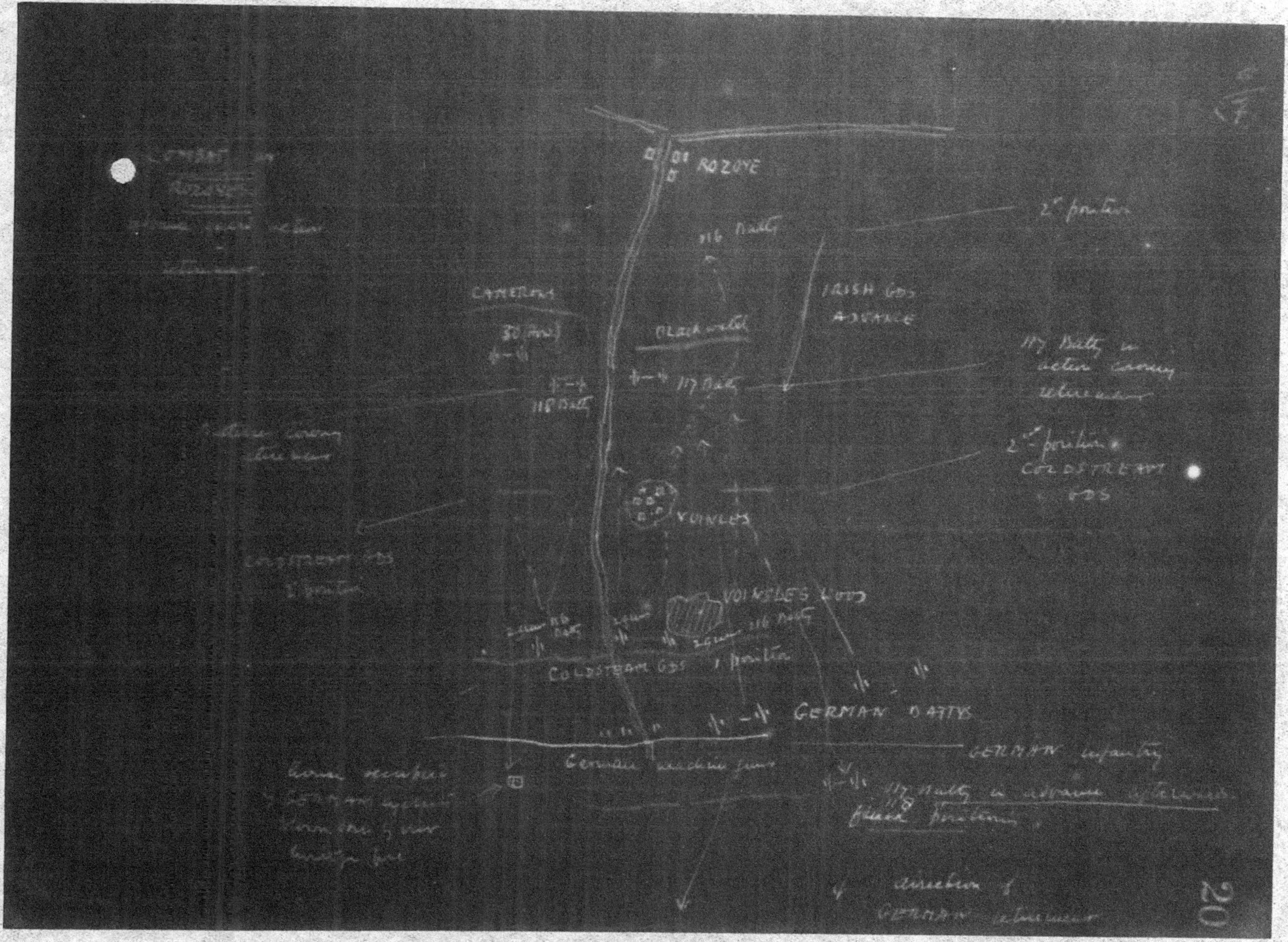

ROZOYE
116 Batty
CAMERONS
Black watch
IRISH GDS
ADVANCE
117 Batty
118 Batty
2nd position
COLDSTREAM
GDS
VOINLES
VOINSLES WOOD
116 Batty
COLDSTREAM GDS 1 position
GERMAN BATTYS
GERMAN infantry
German machine guns
20

21

COMBAT on
BILLOT
26. 3 de staff rides on
killed in action (?)

March centered
of Germans.

SMALVILLERE
Third woods hilly
Tagen

Cannons &
Altace Watch cleared these woods
lost 30 prisoners

GERMAN BATTERIES

BILLOT

ourselfs
front
115 Regt

where German flash,
Colonel & killed way
known site

No 1/4 116 Batty
came in time

over + broken lorry

French Cavalry 118 Batty
H.A. McClintock Major Julian

22

○ CHIMNEY GERMAN Obs. station

CHEMIN DE DAMES

← AILLES
German M.G.
woodyard

Direction of GERMAN GUNS

British dugouts

GERMAN FIRE

16th Batln. Fr'ch H.Q.
18 Batn. to relieve

117 Batn. relieve
2 Clearing Station 26 M.E.

Queens shed

TOUR DE PAISSY
35 Batn. relieve

Bivouac on 17 Sept.

team convoy

Bivouac on 16 Sept.

26 (heavy) Divn.

TOUR DE PAISSY

Bivouac on 18 Sept.

N—R 16 M.E.
I-phine 16 Sept.
First enemy rifle
fire MSNE
heavy fighting 16–26 Sept.
rested for 10 or 12 days.

Arrived 16th / JUMILLY

22

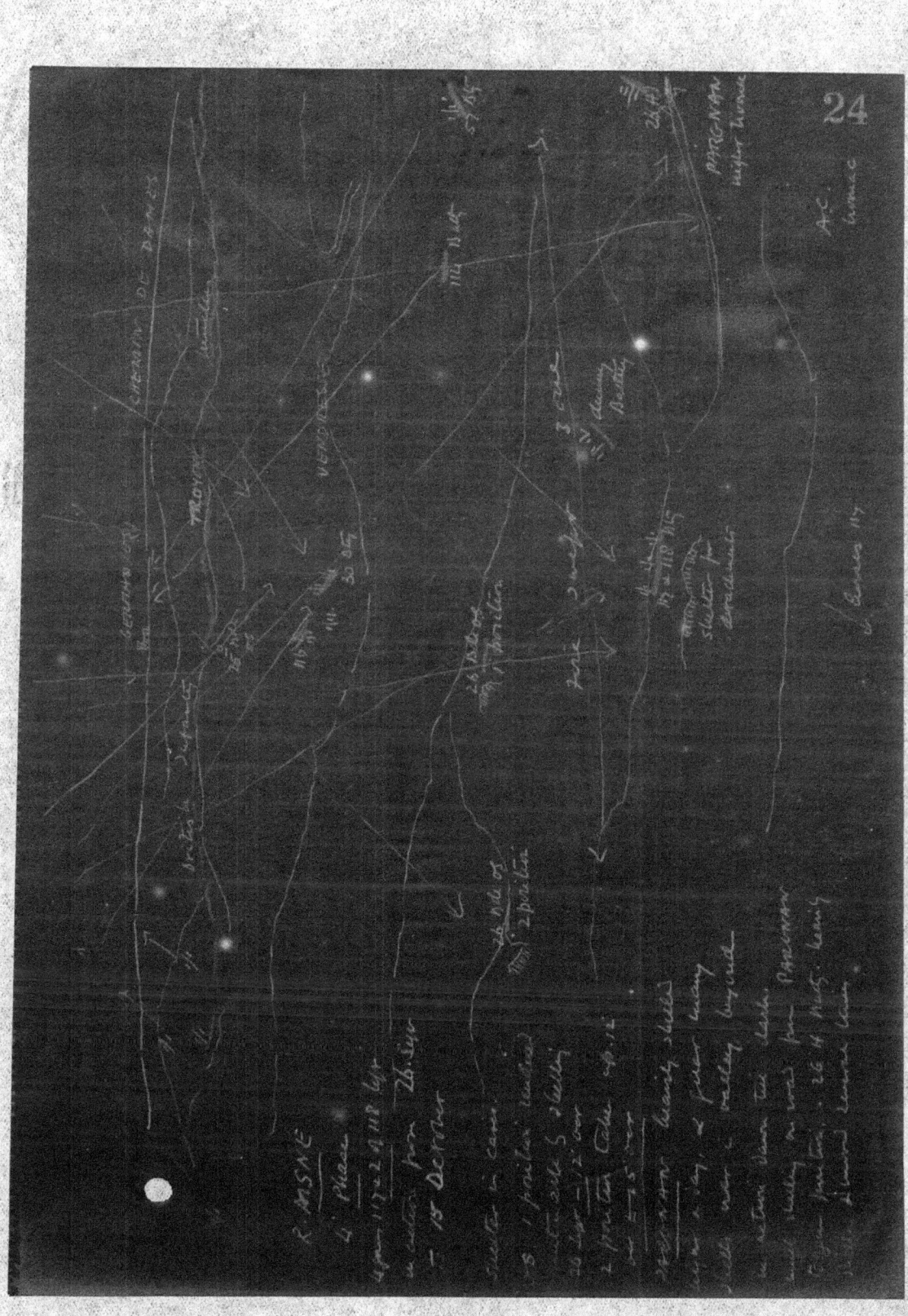

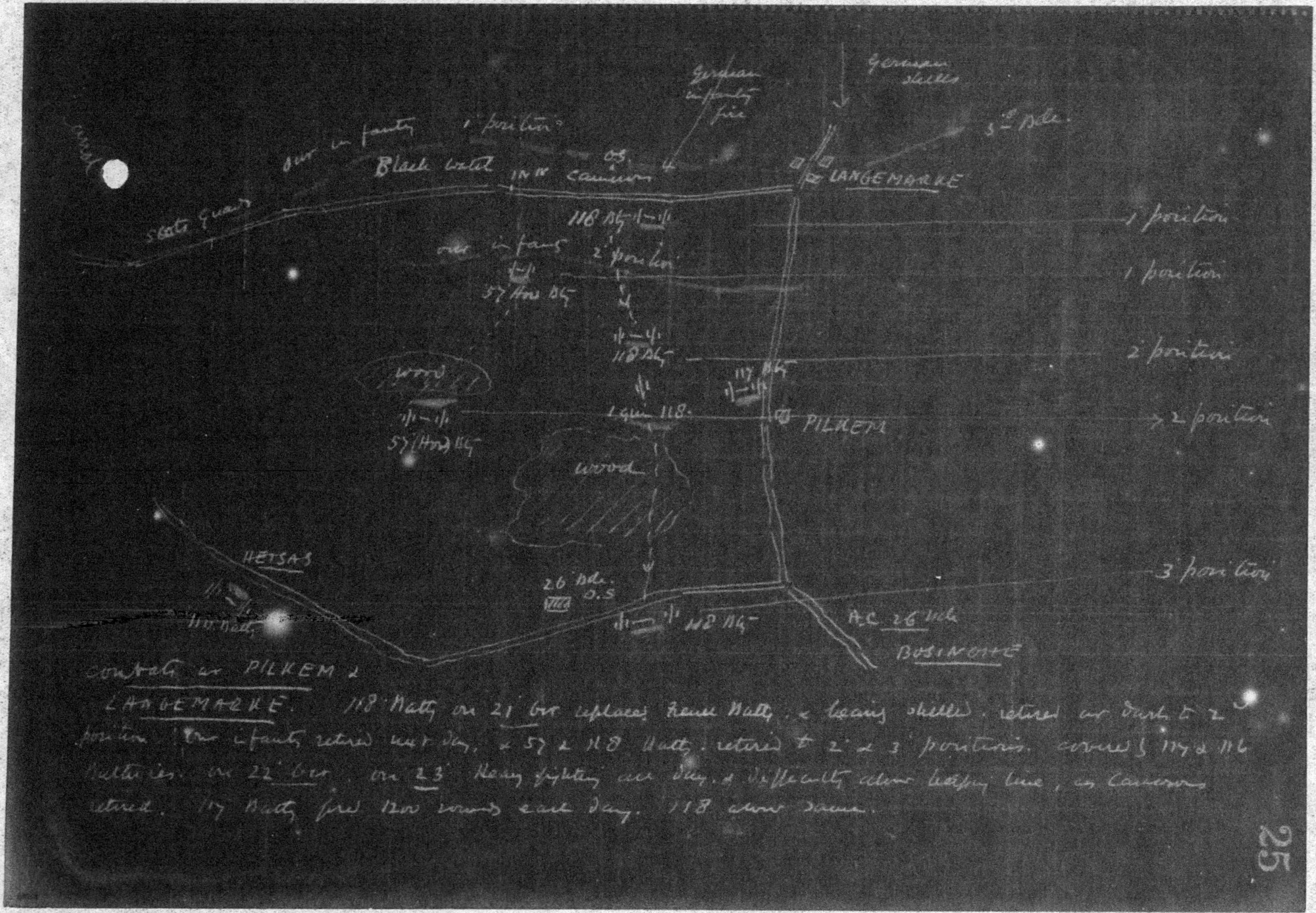
German infantry fire
German shells
3rd Bde.
LANGEMARKE
1 position
1 position
2 position
2 position
3 position
PILKEM
Black Watch
INN
Camerons
O.S.
Scots Guards
our infantry
118 Bty
2 position
57 How Bty
118 Bty
117 Bty
1 gun 118
wood
57 (How) Bty
wood
26 Bde.
O.S.
118 Bty
HETSAS
R.C. 26 Bde
BOESINGHE
Contacts at PILKEM & LANGEMARKE. 118 Batty on 21 Oct replaced French Batty & being shelled retired at dusk to 2 position. Our infantry retired next day, & 57 & 118 Batts retired to 2 & 3 positions covering 117 & 116 batteries on 22 Oct. On 23 Heavy fighting all day & difficulty about keeping line, as Camerons retired. 117 Batty fired 1200 rounds each day. 118 about same.
25

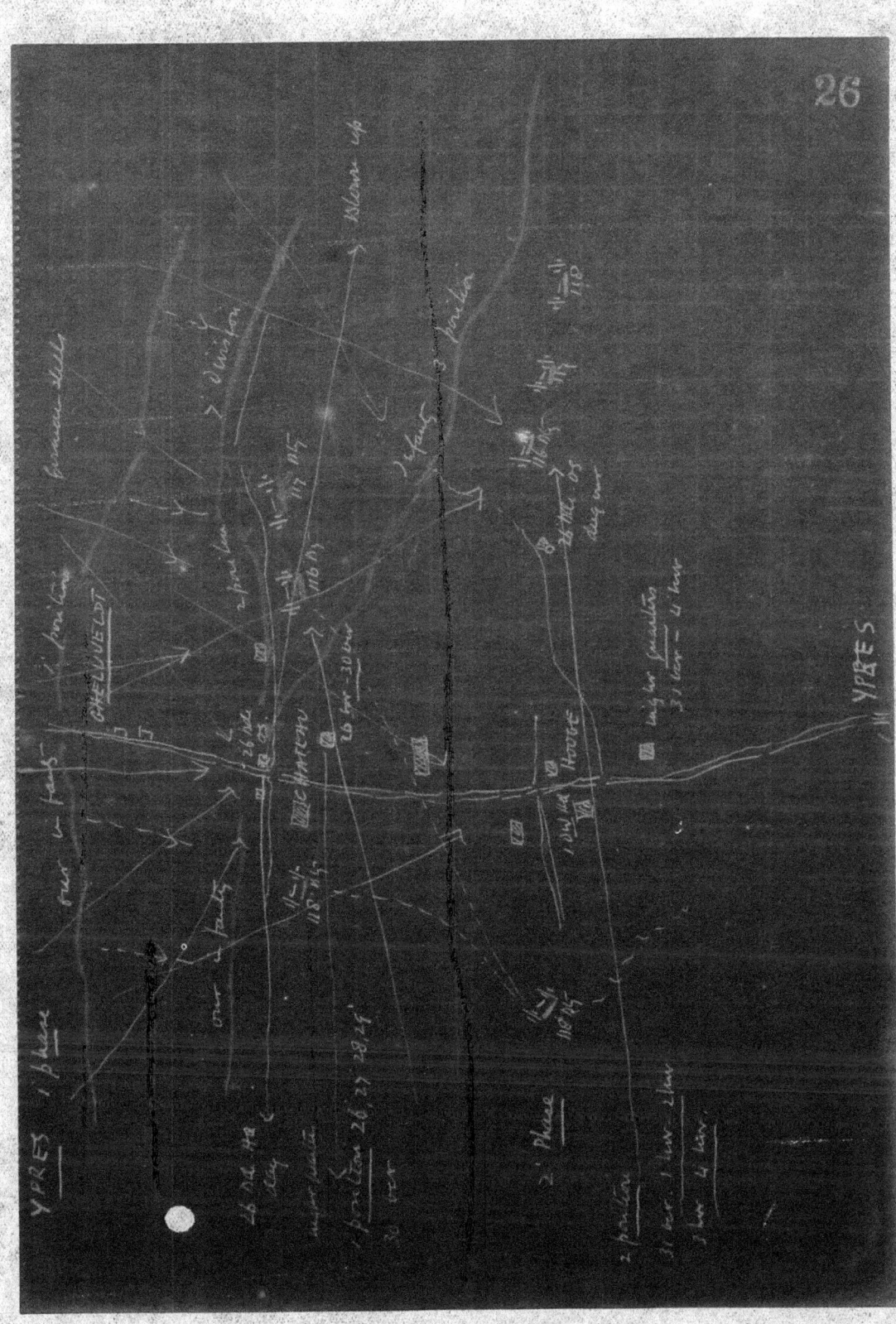

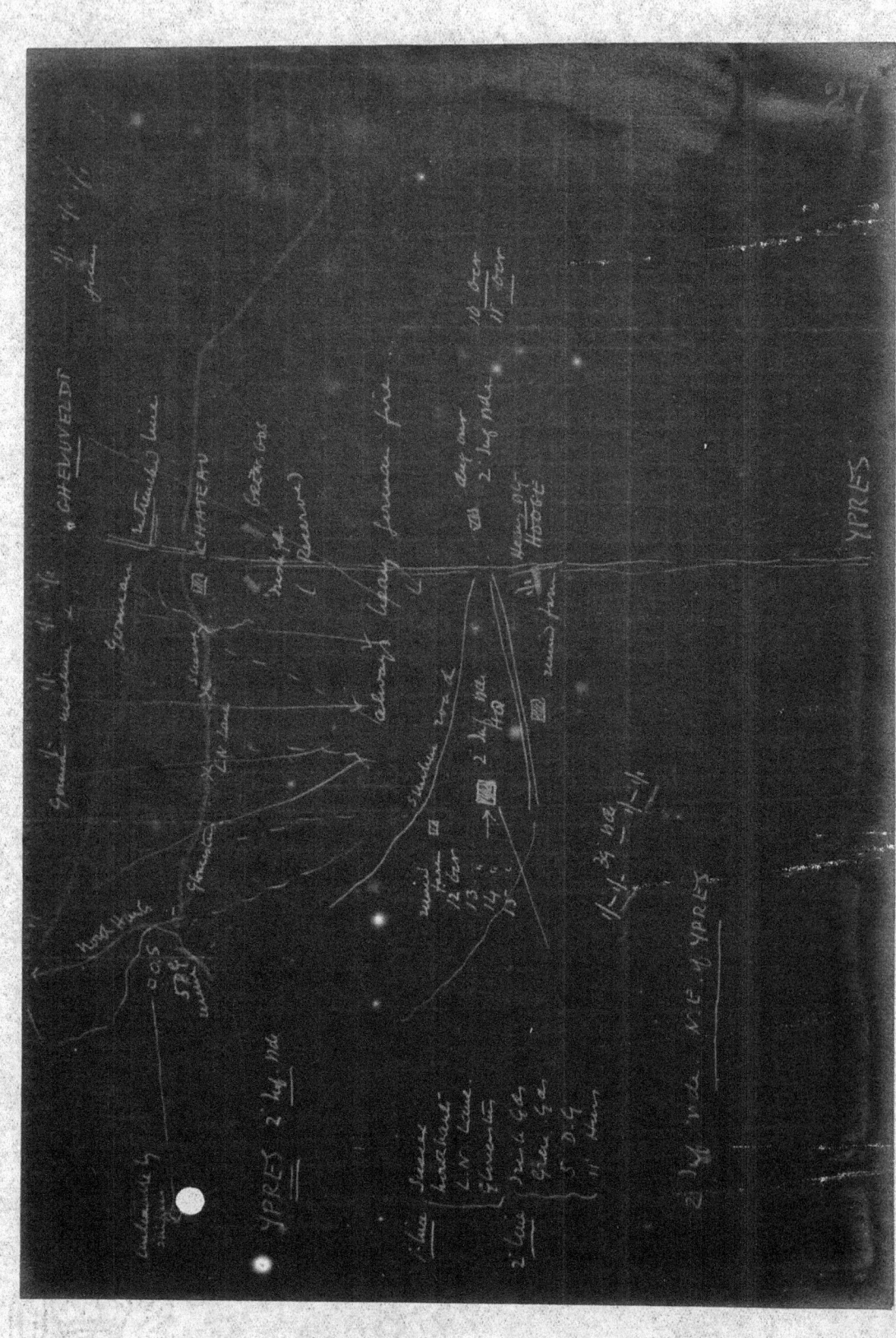

XXVI RA

1st Div. B.E.F
1914.

From
Brken (Lieut. Col.)
Cunliffe Owen, RFA.

1st Division

WAR DIARY

XXVI BRIGADE   R. F. A.

October

1914

Army Form C. 2118.

WAR DIARY
or
INTELLIGENCE SUMMARY
(Erase heading not required.)

Instructions regarding War Diaries and Intelligence Summaries are contained in F.S. Regs., Part II. and the Staff Manual respectively. Title pages will be prepared in manuscript.

Place	Hour, Date	Summary of Events and Information	Remarks and references to Appendices
PILKEM	22.10.14.		
	10 a.m.	117 in action 400 x N of PILKEM against troops bivouac N.E. of INN.	
	10.30 a.m.	57ᵗʰ Hows By panicked with 28ᵗʰ R.B⁻	
	11.30 a.m.	118 in action ½ mile N.W. of PILKEM. On PILKEM–INN road against Battery near MANGELAERE	
	3 p.m.	Enemy made strong attack on INN. On infantry in front of 118 retired to 118 withdrew to	
		position 20 – 1 mile W. of PILKEM	
		Batteries engaged rest of day against infantry. Remained in position at night. Except	
		57. 15.G withdrawn to PILKEM.	
	23.10.14		
	6.15 a.m.	As soon as 118 pushed forward km road junction S.E. of INN to try & obtain	
		direct fire on INN which has in hands of enemy. This was not possible but	
		hill just E. of INN was destroyed.	
		118 withdrawn 400 x S. of former position	OR
		Other batteries as before.	118 2 wounded
	12.45 p.m	28 B⁴ & 57ᵗʰ Battery placed under orders of R.U.C. 2ⁿᵈ Bdᵗ.	
	"	117 turned on to trench reported by infantry just N. of road junction ½ mile	
		W. of LANGEMARCKE STA.	
	1 p.m.	57 & 118 shelling at road junction just N.W. of INN with aeroplane reconnaissance reported effective.	
	1.15 p.m.	116 shelling at enemies batteries near MERSANDENNI with aeroplane.	
	3.30 p.m.	118 in action about 1000 x N. of MANGELAERE	
		116 on battery at ½ mile S.G.E. of Y-ER BRANDE INNIS.	
	5 p.m.	Enemy attacked INN 118 & 116 firing N. of INN.	
	7.30 p.m.	Snip Sec. of 118 withdrawn to join battery	
	8.15 p.m.	116 on road junction N.W. of INN. Batteries remained in position.	

Forms/C. 2118/10

Army Form C. 2118.

WAR DIARY
or
INTELLIGENCE SUMMARY.
(Erase heading not required.)

26 Res. Rfa

Instructions regarding War Diaries and Intelligence Summaries are contained in F.S. Regs., Part II. and the Staff Manual respectively. Title pages will be prepared in manuscript.

Hour, Date, Place		Summary of Events and Information	Remarks and references to Appendices
24.10.14 PILKEM	7 a.m.	117 firing N.E. of INN	
	9.30 a.m.	116 on battery reported by infantry 500 x N.E. INN	
	11.30 a.m.	118 in direct reaching N.E. of INN	
	12.15 p.m.	118 on K.7/KORTEBEEK with aeroplane reconnaissance	
	12.45 p.m.	57 on battery 500 x N.E. INN	
	2 p.m.	118 on battery 500 x N.E. INN	
	7 p.m.	116 with drawn Dranoutre E. ZILLEBEKE	
	7.45 p.m.	Enemy attacks 117, 118 & 57 all firing	
25.10.14	2 a.m.	118 marches to ZILLEBEKE	
	5 a.m.	117	
ZILLEBEKE 26.10.14	4.45 a.m.	57 under orders of 43rd I.B.de	
		Left ZILLEBEKE with 15th I.B.de. 57 How B.3 grouped with 26 I.B.de	116 1 S.R. wounded
	9 a.m.	57 in action about 2 of VELDHOEK against POEZEHOEK	
	11 a.m.	117 in action just S.of 8th Div. Stans E of GHELUVELT against enemy trenches N of RK	
		REIDEBEEK forward observing officer	
	12.30 p.m.	115 in action at V of VELDHOEK against trenches S.E. ZUIDHOEK	117 1 O.R. wounded
	4 p.m.	116 at F.M. GHELUVELT	
		117 withdrawn to position W of 116	
		Same position	
27.10.14	10 a.m.	118 in battery about I of ZUIDHOEK	

26. N.R. RFA

WAR DIARY
or
INTELLIGENCE SUMMARY.
(Erase heading not required.)

Army Form C. 2118.

Hour, Date, Place	Summary of Events and Information	Remarks and references to Appendices
27.10.14. 11.45 a.m.	116 on 4 gun battery 500 x E of 10 Km stone on MENIN YPRES	with aeroplane
11.50 a.m.	118 on 8 " in angle of main crossroad 500 x W of B of BECELAERE	
11.55 a.m.	57 on 4 " 1500 yds S.W. of J of TERHAND	reconnaissance
12 noon	117 on 4 " " at H of WESTHOEK	
	Batteries shelled above teams throughout the afternoon	
28.10.14. 9.30 a.m.	57 on battery in angle of main rd W of BECELAERE	
"	116 " " at J of ZUIDHOEK	Supporting 2nd Division attack on REUTEL
"	117 Searching ground between REUTEL – NORD WEST HOER – BECELAERE	
"	118 on wood between BECELAERE & W of NORD WEST HOER & in woods tending E	
11 a.m.	57 rejoin 42nd Bde R.F.A.	
2 p.m.	116 on Lorry Lines 500 yds N.E. of fig 10 on MENIN – YPRES Rd.	116 O.R. 1 wounded
2.30 p.m.	118 Shooting Trench 200 x N.S.W. of WESTHOER to support 6th Bde.	
2.45 p.m.	117 South of Wood REUTEL	117 3 wounded
5 p.m.	116 turn for night on trenches running N from fig 10 on YPRES – MENIN Rd. for 500 yds	
29.10.14. 5.30 a.m.	German attack against our trenches at cross roads at 9th Km YPRES – MENIN Rd. under fire 1st B.A. Major Stokes German attack was repulsed on line 9th Km. ZANDVOORDE 118 Capt. Sinclair wounded 3 batteries were to fire on enemys trenches just in front of infantry which had to be allowed to come on. German attack was known made N of MENIN YPRES Rd. 116 on battery at NORD WEST HOER W of BECELAERE	
	118	
7.30 a.m.	all batteries searching from BECELAERE to YPRES – MENIN Rd.	

C. Cuncliffe Owen
Col. 26 N.R. RFA

WAR DIARY
or
INTELLIGENCE SUMMARY.
(Erase heading not required.)

Army Form C. 2118.

Instructions regarding War Diaries and Intelligence Summaries are contained in F.S. Regs., Part II. and the Staff Manual respectively. Title pages will be prepared in manuscript.

Hour, Date, Place	Summary of Events and Information	Remarks and references to Appendices
29.10.14. 8.45 a.m.	Enemy reported massing N.E. 9 Km. Shri. All batteries searching there.	
11 a.m.	Counter attack by 3rd 15th on left. Shells YPRES-MENIN Rd. all batteries firing E of Ypres at enemy & through POEZELHOEK.	
30.10.14. 2 a.m.	German div. track of artillery along road running N. from 9 Km. All batteries on the road & the wood just S of POEZELHOEK. Same lines for night.	
8 a.m.	Order from 1st S.A. Hqrs. here to bombard as under. Heavy bombardment by firmans. Batteries fired steady fire as follows — 116 500x N 0 10 Km against battery. 117 on battery at H.M. NORDWESTHOEK 118 made fire of heavy Hows & Could not hear the firers.	117 2 Weken killed. 118 11 O.R. wounded.
8.20 a.m.	Bombardment Ceases. Very little firing on our front all day.	
3 p.m.	118, 117 (with high explosive) a german wanning or himself S.B. POEZIE HOEK. 118 on about target. 117 1 Battin E. road running N from 9 Km. Battery 500 x N.W. of BECELAERE	
	116 on Guns road at 9 Km.	
31.10.14. 6.15 a.m.	Fire on follows ordered by 1st S.A. Guns on shown except 116 who had 1 section on battery 500 x N.E. 10 Km. 200 x N.E. 9.10 Km.	

(9 29 6) W 3332—1107 100,000 10/13 H W V Forms/C. 2118/16.

Army Form C. 2118.

WAR DIARY
or
INTELLIGENCE SUMMARY.
(Erase heading not required.)

26 Inf. Bde.

Instructions regarding War Diaries and Intelligence Summaries are contained in F.S. Regs., Part II. and the Staff Manual respectively. Title pages will be prepared in manuscript.

Hour, Date, Place		Summary of Events and Information	Remarks and references to Appendices
ZILLEBEKE 31.10.14	10 a.m.	Our infantry & bomb cops shelled out of their trenches & had to retire. 116, 117, 118 evening retirement.	116. O.R. 7 wounded
			117. 1 killed 15 wounded.
	2 pm	26 Bde ordered to retake to position N. of WESTHOEK	118. Wt. Fletcher killed
		11 P.R. ordered to attack by night their	O.R. 1 killed 5 wounded
	9.30 pm	orders to move to position 1 mile E. of ZILLEBEKE	movement suspended

C. Smith Bt
Col.
10/11/14
Col 26 Inf. Bde

Army Form C. 2118

WAR DIARY
or
INTELLIGENCE SUMMARY.

(Erase heading not required.)

Instructions regarding War Diaries and Intelligence Summaries are contained in F. S. Regs., Part II. and the Staff Manual respectively. Title pages will be prepared in manuscript.

Place	Date	Hour	Summary of Events and Information	Remarks and references to Appendices

1st Division.

WAR DIARY

XXVI BRIGADE R.F.A.

November

1914.

Army Form C. 2.

WAR DIARY
or
INTELLIGENCE SUMMARY.
(Erase heading not required.)

Instructions regarding War Diaries and Intelligence Summaries are contained in F.S. Regs., Part II. and the Staff Manual respectively. Title pages will be prepared in manuscript.

26 Nov 14

Hour, Date, Place	Summary of Events and Information	Remarks and references to Appendices
31.10.14 10 a.m.	Our infantry S.E. Kelen road shelled & left their trenches retired to	OR 116 7 W 117 1 K 15 W " 2/Lt Fickbeck OR ae. 1K 8 W
2 pm	32 A Bde ordered to relieve 1 Bns G.HW WESTHOEK	
9.30 pm	Ordered to move to position 1 mile S.of ZILLEBEKE	
1.11.14 4 am	All batteries in position E of road through E of ZILLEBEKE. Engaged enemy batteries by lamp Busses 7 and HOOGE	1 hour wounded B/118 battery
8.30	Ordered by 1st Div'n to be attached to line of 3rd Bde. 2/sec F/116 entrenched 200 yds SE of X roads on YPRES-MENIN road	
2.11.14	Ordered to support 2nd Bde. 1/Bde. relies 1 sec on trenches between 2 roads 177 and 070780	7 men missing B/116 battery. 1 man wounded B/118 " "
2 pm	Batteries engages along searching house S.W. of 2nd Bde line	
8 pm	3rd Bde line driven in 1 2 guns of 116 lost	
12 am	Orders to send 2 more guns into infantry line	
3.11.14	2 guns 116 entrenched 100 yds SOP VELD HOEK	
	Support of 2nd Bde to hour over from 3rd Div. Arts.	
1.30	Section 118 sent in Wednesday when 26 15 Bde. 6 Appt 2 B By /Bde. to trees on enemy in famous french trench GROENENBURG Fm.	6 men wounded B 118 Battery. 2 men missing A 118 battery.
4.11.14	117 + 118 in action when in front SW of HERELOUGH Attack on 7th Div. Army kept off by these fire Ordered to commence hence until very late long after dark	
5.11.14	Section of 118 sent out to replace section lost & left by friends 116 & 118 fine 117 excellent	G. Cart Markwall Lt.Col R.HA

(9 29 6) W 3332—1107 100,000 10/13 H W V Forms/C. 2118/10.

Army Form C. 2118.

WAR DIARY
or
INTELLIGENCE SUMMARY.
(Erase heading not required.)

Instructions regarding War Diaries and Intelligence Summaries are contained in F.S. Regs., Part II. and the Staff Manual respectively. Title pages will be prepared in manuscript.

Hour, Date, Place		Summary of Events and Information	Remarks and references to Appendices
PARGNAN	1.10.14.	4 guns 117 & 2 guns 118 entrenched 400ˣ W. of PARGNAN 116 still in g ordure bef. Mooring under O.C. 25th Bde Lieut ? as above	Casualties 117 9 OR killed 6.10.14 115 1 O.R. wounded 12.10.14 118 1 O.R — 19.10.14 117 3 OR injured 12.10.14
	1.10.14 — 14.10.14		
	16.10.14 10 p.m.	Marched to LOUPEIGNE	
	16.10.14 12.15 a.m.	Reached billets ca. 15/10/14	
		Marched to FÈRE-EN-TARDENOIS	
FÈRE-EN-TARDENOIS	18.10.14 2 a.m.	Entrained	via ST DENIS ETAPLES
	18.10.14 5 a.m.	Left Station	
HAZEBROUCK	17.10.14 12.30 p.m.	Detrained. Delayed for 8 hours by accident on line at BOULOGNE	
	18.10.14	Rested. 116 116 Battery reported	OR 1 missing 18.10.14
	19.10.14 6 a.m.		
	20.10.14 8.45 a.m.	Marched to POPPERINGHE arrived 6 p.m.	
	21.10.14	Left POPPERINGHE, marched via ELVERDINGHE to BOESINGHE & later	117 Lt SOUTHEY wounded 21.10.14 52 Lt LAMBERT wounded
LANGEMARCK		till 12 noon	
	1 p.m.	112 in action just S.G of LANGEMARCKE STA against infantry	
	2.30 p.m.	German attack reported from direction of BIXSCHOOTE 116 & 117 in observation	
	6 p.m.	Just N. of PILKEN facing N.W. Batteries withdrawn to PILKEN.	
PILKEM	22.10.14 7 a.m.	116 Battery in observation at 2½ S.B. HETSAS	
	9 a.m.	116 Battery in action at 12ˢ S.C. HETSAS against infantry N.G. INW	116 OR 1 wounded

Army Form C. 2118.

26th Bde R.F.A.

WAR DIARY
or
INTELLIGENCE SUMMARY.
(Erase heading not required.)

Instructions regarding War Diaries and Intelligence Summaries are contained in F.S. Regs., Part II. and the Staff Manual respectively. Title pages will be prepared in manuscript.

Hour, Date, Place	Summary of Events and Information	Remarks and references to Appendices
6.11.14. 2a.m.	Left Dickebusche. Marched to Hazebrouck to refit with the 26th Bde & 57th Battery.	
6–12.11.14	Refitting at Caghill took over the 26 B⁴ B⁴ on the 11.11.14. At Division going to the 2nd Div Brd on the 9.11.14	
12.11.14.	Left Hazebrouck marched towards Hooge but were turned back to Vlamertinghe an attack was expected.	1 man injured 117 Battery.
13.11.14 12 Mdt	Left Vlamertinghe to take new positions from the 22nd Bde & F Battery. 116 K 12 c & d, 117 K 12 b, 118 K 17 a	Reference map YPRES (sheet 2.8)
14.11.14.	3 rounds fired 118 K22 c & d, 117 K24 c & d, 116 K23 c & d in support of 2nd Caveren Division.	1 man wounded 116 Battery.
15.11.14.	118 fired in trenches in K22 c & d, 116 & 117 fired in woods in their zone. No attack during day.	
16.11.14.	Lt Col Heath took over from Lt Col Coghill. Batteries fired on same zone.	
17.11.14.	117th Battery had 2 guns covering period in the 39th & 13th Brigades. Heavy attack by enemy's infantry in morning & afternoon, all batteries fired. Estl. enemy 116 & 117 hurd.	2 men killed 6 the 116th Battery. 3 men wounded " " 1 man wounded " 117 "
18.11.14	Quiet day: 117 had 400" F G R⁴ Position, 116 hrs North of the YPRES–MENIN Road. batteries in same line.	
19.11.14.	Quiet day, fired to return in last day.	
20.11.14	Handed over to Frenck, 118 badly shelled in afternoon, battens vacated position 6 P.M. were to march through L. I Corps billet but marched spent night on road just W. of WESTOUTRE.	
21.11.14	Marched into billeting area W. of STRAZEELE, arrived 3 P.M.	
30.11.14	Lt Gonville P. Bromhead ... 26.11.14	C. Bromhead Lt Col Comg 26 Bde RFA

1st Division.

WAR DIARY

XXVI BRIGADE R.F.A.

December

1914

1st Division.

WAR DIARY

<u>XXVI BRIGADE AMMUNITION COLUMN. R.F.A.</u>

<u>August</u>

<u>1914</u>

Army Form C. 2118.

WAR DIARY
or
INTELLIGENCE SUMMARY.
(Erase heading not required.)

Instructions regarding War Diaries and Intelligence Summaries are contained in F.S. Regs., Part II. and the Staff Manual respectively. Title pages will be prepared in manuscript.

Hour, Date, Place	Summary of Events and Information	Remarks and references to Appendices
19.12.14	Lt Col G.B. Hinton Takes over the Command of the 26th Bde R.F.A. from Col Cunliffe Owen.	
1 — 23.12.14	Refitting & resting in billeting area W of STRAZEELE.	
23.12.14.	Left billets 9.30 a.m. marched as Div Artillery to BETHUNE, arrived 8 p.m. billeted the night.	
24.12.14.	Left billets early before dawn — 115 in action in P 24 c (North corner)	Rd hds MERVILLE – LA BASSÉE
	117 in action in P 17 d	
	118 in action in P 26 c	
	The 26th Bde supported the 1st Inf Bde. Each battery having an observing station at FESTUBERT. 26th B de HQ opposite L.1380.89 in W.10.a. The 26 Bde Bde HQ bd nr from the 11th Bde (LAHORE) – Battesies unfire livre	
25.12.14.	Batteries fired in support of Infantry. Quiet day for Artillery.	
26.12.14.	Batteries in same positions in Same zones.	
27.12.14.	117 battery in reserve, 116 & 118 batteries support infantry of 1st Bde.	
28.12.14	1st HBde (Gen LOWER STOTTISH & BLACKWATCH) moved into billets in BETHUNE. 26th Bde HQ moved to 2nd Inf Bde. Batteries in same zone – 116 battery in reserve. 117 enfiladed Enemys Trench M.O GIVENCHY 26th BM HQ moved up to canal head GIVENCHY STA.	2/Lt J. Elliott wounded. Other casualties: B g 115 wounded. 1 g 118 wounded.
29.12.14	118 battery in reserve, 117 silenced machine gun. 26th BM HQ moved up to canal head GIVENCHY STA.	
30.12.14	117 in reserve. Batteries registered roads in their front	
31.12.14	116 moved their position west to P22a (NE corner) 116 in reserve, attack during night	

G.B. Hinton Lt Col Cmdg 26 Bde RFA

Army Form C. 2118.

WAR DIARY
or
INTELLIGENCE SUMMARY of 26th Bde Ammn Col. R.F.A.
from 5th August 1914

(Erase heading not required.)

Instructions regarding War Diaries and Intelligence Summaries are contained in F.S. Regs., Part II. and the Staff Manual respectively. Title pages will be prepared in manuscript.

Hour, Date, Place	Summary of Events and Information	Remarks and references to Appendices
6.45 pm 5-8-14 Aldershot N.O.	Capt HARRISON arrived from NEWCASTLE ON TYNE. Packed column vehicles. Completed taking over horses from 26th Bde A.C. Marking begun. Delayed by single dyes for letters & numbered figures. Lt LAMBERT joined.	
6.0 pm 6.8-14 Aldershot N.C.	Completed marking horses. B.S.M. HOWES & 18 N.C.Os & men joined from SHEFFIELD. B.Q.M.S. FOSBURY joined from 116th Battery. Seven A.S.C. drivers joined. Three officers chargers joined. hopay Sergeant caused inconvenience.	
6.10 pm 7.8.14 Aldershot N.C.	3 N.C.Os 15 Gunners joined. 19 Gunners joined from Reserve NEWCASTLE. Harness attempted & identified. Within receptacles 18 pr ammn & present. Knapsack & Reservoir & haversack joined. Lt WURTELE joined.	
6.0 pm 8.8.14	4 N.C.Os 8 gunners 41 drivers joined from NEWCASTLE 4 H.D. horses joined. 2 R 2 LD horses joined field kits inspected. Spare jackets & fur hoods of Reservists handed in. Many men deficient of B64 & identity discs & haversacks. Wheels of carriages painted.	

Army Form C. 2118.

WAR DIARY
or
INTELLIGENCE SUMMARY.

(Erase heading not required.) of 26th Bde Amm Col 7 7

from 5th August 1914

Instructions regarding War Diaries and Intelligence Summaries are contained in F.S. Regs., Part II. and the Staff Manual respectively. Title pages will be prepared in manuscript.

Hour, Date, Place	Summary of Events and Information	Remarks and references to Appendices
6.45 pm 5-8-14 Aldershot N.C.	Capt HARRISON arrived for NEWCASTLE ON TYNE. Packed column vehicles.	
6.0 pm 6-8-14 Aldershot N.C.	Completed taking over horses for 26th Bde Amm Col's. Marking begun. Relayer by single days for letters & figures. LT LAMBERT joined. Completed marking horses. B.S.M. HOWES. & 15 N.C.Os & men joined from SHEFFIELD. BQMS. FOSBURY joined from 116 Battery. Seven A.S.C. horses joined. Three officers chargers joined. ½ a pay sergeant & men issue here	
4.0 pm 7-8-14 Aldershot N.C.	3 N.C.O. 15 gunners 19 drivers joined from Reserve NEWCASTLE. Harness assembled & ditted. Wicker receptacles 18 pr amm² packed. Men paid + Reservist Statemen joined. Lt WURTELE joined.	
6.0 pm 8-8-14 Aldershot N.C.	4 N.C.Os 8 gunners 41 drivers joined from NEWCASTLE. N.H.D 2 R. 2 L.D. horses joined. Field kits inspected. Spare parts upper boots of Reservists handed in. Many men deficient of B.Ms, identity discs & various kits of clothing.	
9-8-14 Aldershot	General	
10-8-14 "	Drawing horses from Remount Dept. Training	
11-8-14 Aldershot	Remounts in charge	
12- "	Parade in F.S. Marching Order + route march	
13- "	Marching also completed	
14- Aldershot	Route Marching daily 8 miles	
15- "	14-8-14. Practice supply of ammunition with Brigade.	
16-8-14 Southampton	Embarked on S.S. Carlyrushire at Southampton	
17-8-14 Boulogne	Disembarked at Boulogne. Marched to Rest Camp.	

WAR DIARY
or
INTELLIGENCE SUMMARY.
(Erase heading not required.)

Army Form C. 2118.

Hour, Date, Place	Summary of Events and Information	Remarks and references to Appendices
18-8-14 Boulogne	Remained in Rest Camp.	
19-8-14 Boulogne	9.30 pm Completed entraining & left.	
20-8-14 Boué	Detrained at Le Nouvion, marched to Boué.	
21-8-14 Boué	Halted.	
21-8-14 Cartignies	Marched Cartignies.	
22-8-14 Line of March	from Cartignies – Maubeuge – Grand Reng.	
23-8-14 Grand Reng	Marched at night to Lameries.	
24-8-14.	In action at Bettignies. Supplied 115 R'ds & 10 R'ds Ammn. Oilstead hostilities at end of day. Marched to Longueville	
25-8-14	Marched to Dompierre	
26-8-14	Marched to Pont-au-Cambrecis. Position in action taken near OPAN & FAYT. Munitions supplied. Column split. Heavy Company left 1½ miles to rear.	
27-8-14 Pont-au-Cambrecis	Remained with SAA at Pont of Rear for action through Etreux & Guise. Bivouacked Jonqueuses.	Lt. Lambert joins 118th R.F.A.
28-8-14 } St Gobain	Marched to St. Gobain	
29-8-14 }	Halted.	

Army Form C. 2118.

Copy. Original to Sept. Wy

WAR DIARY
or
INTELLIGENCE SUMMARY.
(Erase heading not required.)

Instructions regarding War Diaries and Intelligence Summaries are contained in F.S. Regs., Part II. and the Staff Manual respectively. Title pages will be prepared in manuscript.

Hour, Date, Place	Summary of Events and Information	Remarks and references to Appendices
30.8.14 ALLEMANT	Marched to ALLEMANT	
31-8-14	Marched to high ground S. of Soissons	

1st Division.

WAR DIARY

XXVI BRIGADE AMMUNITION COLUMN. R.F.A.

September

1914.

Army Form C. 2118.

WAR DIARY
or
INTELLIGENCE SUMMARY.
(Erase heading not required.)

2 Bde Amm Column
September 1914

Hour, Date, Place	Summary of Events and Information	Remarks and references to Appendices
30-8-14 ALLEMANT	Marched to ALLEMANT	
31-8-14 —	Marched through pouring S. of SOISSONS	
1-9-14 —	Marched to LA FERTÉ MILON. Section of Amm'n Col with Rear Guard. 11.0pm Marched to MEAUX	
2pm 2-9-14 MEAUX	arrived 10.30 a.m. 2-9-14. Halted at MEAUX.	
3-9-14 —	Rejoined Brigade at LA FERTÉ SOUS JOUARRE	
4-9-14 COULOMMIERS	Marched to COULOMMIERS. Pursued in evening S. Column under Lt WURTELE took a heavy section.	
5-9-14 —	Marched to NESLE. Lt WURTELE other types with heavy section	
6-9-14	Lt WURTELE + section rejoin. March to ROZOY. 8 A.M. Here. 116 Bty refitted ammunition. Amm's to 1st Bde + 117 Bty. Bivouacked with 21st Bde + PUISEAUX. Bivouaced.	
7-9-14	Advanced with 1st Bde + turned at LE FRENOIS near CHOISY. Column shelled again	

Army Form C. 2118.

WAR DIARY
or
INTELLIGENCE SUMMARY.
(Erase heading not required.)

Instructions regarding War Diaries and Intelligence Summaries are contained in F.S. Regs., Part II. and the Staff Manual respectively. Title pages will be prepared in manuscript.

Hour, Date, Place	Summary of Events and Information	Remarks and references to Appendices
8-9-14	Marched with Advanced gd. Shelled from A/c taking position for Batteries, 2 horses hit. Short action. Regt 11th Ft Battery. Marched to Firmine at HONDVILLIERS via SABLONNIÈRES	
9.9.14	Marched to LANOUETTE FM. Bivouac there	
10.9.14	4 miles N of SAULCHERY. N of the R. MARNE. Brigade in action at FOURCHANAS, Column Kept touch in advance. Bivouac at LATICCY	
11.9.14	Marched to TRUGNY. Waited for	
12.9.14	Marched to BAZOCHES. Waited for	
13.9.14	Marched to BOURG. Bridge over RAISNE destroyed. Stone Canal Bridge. Shelled at long range on River bank. Bivouac at BOURG.	
14.9.14	Marched with 2nd Attack Army to High ground near TOUR DE PAISSY M.E. BOURG. Supplied Ammn to 2nd Bde at VENDRESSE also to Batteries 117—118 on Ridge N. TOUR-DE-PAISSY. HQ at TROYON. Bivouac ARBRE-DE-PAISSY	

Army Form C. 2118.

WAR DIARY
or
INTELLIGENCE SUMMARY.
(Erase heading not required.)

Instructions regarding War Diaries and Intelligence Summaries are contained in F.S. Regs., Part II. and the Staff Manual respectively. Title pages will be prepared in manuscript.

Hour, Date, Place	Summary of Events and Information	Remarks and references to Appendices
15.9.14.	Between 1st Echelon in position near 117th Battery. Heavily shelled about a few by H.E. Behind behind TOUR-DE-PAISSY. Supplied ammn as before.	Received wagon 2 wh limber & from VENDRESSE & wounded men by H.E. Shell.
16.9.14	Proceeded behind to TOUR-DE-PAISSY. Newton had prisoner in position. TOUR-DE-PAISSY. Supplied. Remained in position.	
17.9.14 JUMIGNY	Battling with amn in new position. Vectte but Bivouac on Position. Same Position. Supplied batteries as usual went to find Found filled to Brigade in JUMIGNY. Bivouac. all day. Moved in at Dark shelled.	
18.9.14	Same position. Batteries supplied as usual. shelled.	
3.30 am – 19.9.14	Enemy made a night attack repulsed. Return in position Batteries in taps JUMIGNY to S. JUMIGNY on Road. at night. Shelled.	
20.9.14 JUMIGNY	Column in position 1st S of JUMIGNY. Heavily shelled all day. A few horses hit. Rattis as usual.	
21-9-14	Same as 20th-9-14	

WAR DIARY
or
INTELLIGENCE SUMMARY.
(Erase heading not required.)

Army Form C. 2118.

Instructions regarding War Diaries and Intelligence Summaries are contained in F.S. Regs., Part II. and the Staff Manual respectively. Title pages will be prepared in manuscript.

Hour, Date, Place	Summary of Events and Information	Remarks and references to Appendices
22-9-14 JUMIGNY	Same as 21-9-14. Heavily shelled	Several men suffering from shock, attacks repulsed, not grave on their whole.
23-9-14 —	Same as 22-9-14 "	
24-9-14 —	Same as 23-9-14. Some removals formed.	Lt. HURTEL E 10mm battery 26/9/14 (iii)
25-9-14 PARGNAN	Withdrew at day break to PARGNAN, shelled about 4pm to 8am 26/9/14 by heavy howitzers.	2/Lt. RUSHER 10mm 2nd zelder 24/9/14
26-9-14 —	6am. Concealed column from aircraft. All guns 2nd zelder shelled at camp at OEUILLY	2/Lt RUNER 10mm 1st zelder 24/9/14
27-9-14 —	Same position all quiet	
28-9-14 – 30-9-14 —	Same position. Some Shrapnel burst over camp	
1-10-14		
2-10-14	Same position all quiet	

1st Division.

WAR DIARY

XXVI BRIGADE AMMUNITION COLUMN. R.F.A.

October

1914.

Army Form C. 2118.

"1/26 Bar Amm Colum"

Copy. Original with
Septr War Diary

WAR DIARY
or
INTELLIGENCE SUMMARY.
(Erase heading not required.)

Instructions regarding War Diaries and Intelligence Summaries are contained in F.S. Regs., Part II. and the Staff Manual respectively. Title pages will be prepared in manuscript.

Hour, Date, Place	Summary of Events and Information	Remarks and references to Appendices
FARGNAN		
1/10/14	Same position. Some shrapnel burst over camp.	
2/10/14	Same position all quiet	

Army Form C. 2118.

WAR DIARY
or
INTELLIGENCE SUMMARY.
(Erase heading not required.)

Hour, Date, Place	Summary of Events and Information	Remarks and references to Appendices
3. 10-18 PACQNAN	Some practice. Shelled a/c from Fournes wood	
4.	for 2 hours.	
5.	All quiet	
6.	Shelled Fournes wood for 2 hours.	
7.	Shelled	
8.	All quiet	
9.	All quiet	
10.	All quiet	
11.	Shelled Fournes wood for 2 hours.	
12.	All quiet	
13.	Shelled by trator	
14.	Moved at night to LOUPEIG NE	
15. LOUPEIGNE	Halted at LOUPEIGNE	

Army Form C. 2118.

WAR DIARY
or
INTELLIGENCE SUMMARY.

(Erase heading not required.)

Instructions regarding War Diaries and Intelligence Summaries are contained in F.S. Regs., Part II. and the Staff Manual respectively. Title pages will be prepared in manuscript.

Hour, Date, Place	Summary of Events and Information	Remarks and references to Appendices
16 — 10 — 14 FERE-EN-TARDENOIS	Entrained	
17 CASSEL	DETRAINED. Marched to HAZEBROUK	
18 HAZEBROUK	All quiet	
19 —	—	
20 POPERINGE	Marched to POPERINGHE	
21 PICKEM	Engaged with enemy near LANGEMARCK	
22 —	—	
23 —	—	
24 —	—	
25 —	—	
26 ZILLEBEKE	Marched at night to ZILLE BEKE in 2 Echelon	
27 ½ his S. VELDHOEK	Engaged with enemy. Mytilly killed	

Form C. 2118/10

WAR DIARY
INTELLIGENCE SUMMARY

Army Form C. 2118.

26th Bar RFA Armr Column

Hour, Date, Place	Summary of Events and Information	Remarks and references to Appendices
28-10-14 ½ m. S. VERDHOEK	Engaged with enemy. Slightly shelled	
29. ¾	Moved ½ S. to new position. Engaged with enemy	
30.	Slightly shelled. One man wounded & 5 horses	
31.	Heavily shelled. Brigade retired to W.F. WESTHOEK. Vehicle got out of being frame under fire with great difficulty. F.S. wagons ammy dump in mud. Sgt HEASMAN killed 6 wounded 30 horses killed wounded	

1st Division
26th Bde RF.A.

WAR B DIARY

117th Battery R.F.A.

August

1914

1st Division
26th Bde RF.A.

Army Form C. 2118.

WAR DIARY
or
INTELLIGENCE SUMMARY.
(Erase heading not required.)

Instructions regarding War Diaries and Intelligence Summaries are contained in F. S. Regs., Part II. and the Staff Manual respectively. Title pages will be prepared in manuscript.

Hour, Date, Place	Summary of Events and Information	Remarks and References to Appendices
Midnight 4–5 August	1st day mobilization commenced. Much of the work has been done on previous day in anticipation. Horses inspected.	
August 6th 12.30 P.M.	2nd Day of Mobr. 2 N.C.Os & 19 men joined from Sheffield. 24 horses joined from Newcastle	
August 7th	3rd day of mobilization. No horses were received.	
August 8th	4th day of mobilization. 4 H.D. horses received. Draft of 1 Bomdr, 15 Gunners, 10 drivers (reservists) from No.1 Depôt.	
August 9th	5th day of mobilization. 81 horses received from remount depôt at 4 A.M. ~~temp~~ 2 Bomdrs joined from No.1 Depôt	
August 10th Aug 11th – 15th	6th day of mobilization. mobilising completed. Awaiting orders.	

Army Form C. 2118.

WAR DIARY
or
INTELLIGENCE SUMMARY.
(Erase heading not required.)

Instructions regarding War Diaries and Intelligence Summaries are contained in F. S. Regs., Part II. and the Staff Manual respectively. Title pages will be prepared in manuscript.

Hour, Date, Place	Summary of Events and Information	Remarks and References to Appendices
Aug 16th Aldershot 10.30 A.M. 12.14 P.M.	The Battery left Aldershot in 2 trains and entrained at Southampton in the S.S. "Inventor" Harrison Line.	
Aug 17th At Sea	Arrived Boulogne about 9 a.m, but were not taken into Docks until 5.30 P.M.	
Aug 18th 12.30 A.M.	Completed disembarkation	
1.45 A.M.	Entrained Marched to camp.	
19th 9.50 A.M.	Commenced entraining from No 4 Boulogne. Four hours has been allowed for entraining — much too long.	
1.56 P.M.	Started towards the front.	
20th 1.38 A.M.	Arrived at Etreux and after bivouacking for breakfast marched to billets at Boué	
21st 7.0 A.M.	Left Section marched to Beaurepaire there to join Adv. G.S. of 3rd Inf. Bde.	
8.30 A.M.	Remainder of Batt. marched to CARTIGNY where it was rejoined by the left Section & billeted.	

Army Form C. 2118.

WAR DIARY
or
INTELLIGENCE SUMMARY.
(Erase heading not required.)

Instructions regarding War Diaries and Intelligence Summaries are contained in F.S. Regs., Part II. and the Staff Manual respectively. Title pages will be prepared in manuscript.

Hour, Date, Place	Summary of Events and Information	Remarks and references to Appendices
22-8-1914 Cartigny	Marched at 4.55 A.M to la GARENNE & thence during afternoon and evening to GRAND RENG.	
23-8-1914	Arrived GRAND RENG at 12.30 A.M	
23rd 8 1914	Left Hornu at 7 P.M. to go on outpost duty with Black Watch.	
24th 8-1914	2nd in command with Black Watch. Low in ditch at Villa Sur Nicole but did not open fire. Bivouacked at la Longueville. Made more than to Longueville to Bavay. Bivouacked in Bavay.	
25th 8 1914		
26th-8-1914	Marched with to Pont Cartain	known dead Capt Michel
27th-8-1914 4pm-5.15pm	Marched with Rear Guard & were in action with Black Watch 1 mile S. of Etreux against a German Surprise and 237 rounds late the about 20 minutes were under Rifle & Gun fire Casualties only 2 men & 4 horses Marched to ???	James Phelan

WAR DIARY
or
INTELLIGENCE SUMMARY.

(Erase heading not required.)

Army Form C. 2118.

Hour, Date, Place	Summary of Events and Information	Remarks and references to Appendices
26.8.14.	Had a very long march from La Jonquence to St Quintin. In action several times but no firing.	
29.8	Rested at St Quintin - Heard German driven back by Guise by our Right French Army.	
30.8		
31.8	Marched at 2 a.m. from St Gobain —	

 1st Division
26th Bde R.F.A.

WAR DIARY

117th Battery R.F.A.

September

1914

Army Form C. 2118.

WAR DIARY
or
INTELLIGENCE SUMMARY.
(Erase heading not required.)

Place	Date	Hour	Summary of Events and Information	Remarks and references to Appendices
	1-9	→	arrived COULLOMIERS. Bivouacked in filthy French barracks. Spent night awaiting relief. Marched early.	
	2-9			
	3-9			
	4-9			
	5-9			
	6-9	→	1st day of advance. 2 miles after leaving Camp came in contact with flank guard (estimated 1 battalion of cyclists, some cavalry and a battery) of German force retiring N. Battery came into action near ROZOY, 1 mile W. of VOINLES village & covered retirement of Colchester Guards. Battery fired about 250 rounds.	

WAR DIARY
or
INTELLIGENCE SUMMARY.

(Erase heading not required.)

Army Form C. 2118.

Hour, Date, Place	Summary of Events and Information	Remarks and references to Appendices
6 - 9	Silenced enemy battery almost immediately. Enemy guns again opened later doing considerable damage to Irish Guards 1st & 3rd 2nd Division on our left. But 117 Battery again silenced the enemy who later was off. Casualties only 1 horse hit in spite of both the battery and the teams in rear coming under enemy shell fire. Advanced in the evening to	
7 - 9		
8 - 9		
9 - 9		
10 - 9		
11 - 9		
12 - 9		

WAR DIARY
or
INTELLIGENCE SUMMARY.
(Erase heading not required.)

Army Form C. 2118.

Instructions regarding War Diaries and Intelligence Summaries are contained in F.S. Regs., Part II. and the Staff Manual respectively. Title pages will be prepared in manuscript.

Hour, Date, Place	Summary of Events and Information	Remarks and references to Appendices
13-9-	10th & 1st Gren. Bn crossed the R. AISNE nr BOURG & bivouacked at latter place.	
14-9-	Marched early in dense mist to PAISSY. Gren. Bn heavily engaged with enemy, but our guns unable to help owing to mist. Batt. in day advanced to "Pont de Ste. Anne" came into action, about 1½ miles N of PAISSY. Shelled part of German position about AILLES & N.N.E. PAISSY. In the evening returned to bivouac just N.N. PAISSY.	
15-9-	At dawn took up position just N. of PAISSY - AILLES road about HARCE & PAISSY - & shelled German position on ridge N. of CERNY. About 3 p.m. the battery came under heavy fire from German high explosive guns situated somewhere N. of CERNY. The factory at CERNY was being used as a German hospital & the accuracy of the enemy fire on our battery made it certain that this hospital was being used as an observing station. One of enemy's shells fell in battery between 3rd gun, killing 2 gunners & others more or less severely, and	Killed: Gunner Pooser Gunner Grant Gunner Parnter [?] Wounded: Sergt Bartrip Gunner Polo Wounded slightly: Sergt Phillips Dr. Goodchild

WAR DIARY
or
INTELLIGENCE SUMMARY.
(Erase heading not required.)

Army Form C. 2118.

Hour, Date, Place	Summary of Events and Information	Remarks and references to Appendices
15-9	damaged an ammunition wagon. Another shell completely overturned another wagon. The detachments were taken out eventually under cover of a trench behind the battery, where Lieut: A.T.H. Hayes & 1 man were wounded by another shell. The Battery from then in evening on return	wounded Lt. Hayes
16-9	JUMIGNY - At dawn took up new position near TOUR DE PAISSY FERME and shelled the factory at CERNY & later the slopes N of CHEMIN des DAMES, from which direction the Germans made a counter attack on our trenches. 1 man was wounded by splinter from a shell -	
18-9	Re-occupied same position, battery was shelled again. No casualties.	wounded Major Packard
19-9	Moved position of battery slightly. Battery was shelled again, but no casualties. Major H.N. Packard was severely wounded at his Observing station at a stack 400 yds from battery, by a burst of German shrapnel.	
20-9	The Battery was again severely shelled from front & flank by German H.E. guns. 2/Lieut J.M. Balfour and 5 men wounded. The guns were left in	wounded 2/Lt Balfour Capt Page [illegible]

WAR DIARY
or
INTELLIGENCE SUMMARY.
(Erase heading not required.)

Army Form C. 2118.

Hour, Date, Place	Summary of Events and Information	Remarks and references to Appendices
20-9-	Action as it was impossible to move them in the heavy frost. The shelling continued during the night.	
21-9-	At dawn, when the detachments returned to the guns, the German H.E. again opened fire, partially burying one gun & smashing the trail, & putty another completely out of action, also smashing an ammunition wagon. When this Shelter near the scene, the battery opened fire, at intervals during the day against the wspt N°757 C-R.H.A. Fire was again opened by the Germans on the battery position till nightfall	
22-9-	At dawn 4 guns & 6 wagons were removed (the 2 damaged guns being left with damaged wagon), the battery took up position S.W. of TOUR DE PAISY FERME. Consequently quiet day. Some target engaged.	Major Manley's R.H.A. } joined to WINTER R.F.A. } inclds. } R.F.A.
23-9-	The teams were shelled shortly after leaving bivouac near JUMIGNY. 1 horse kd. Killed (WOOLFORD). The battery was again heavily shelled all day by H.E. guns & shrapnel. 4 men were wounded at night. Battery moved to another position 500 yds south.	* killed — Lr Woolford, wounded — Pte O'Connor
24-9-	Battery position apparently not located by enemy but visibly open	

WAR DIARY or INTELLIGENCE SUMMARY

Army Form C. 2118.

Hour, Date, Place	Summary of Events and Information	Remarks and references to Appendices
24-9	heavily shelled. 1 man (McLeod) killed. In evening Battery was relieved by 51st Battery R.F.A. and removed at dawn to height of PARGNAN. Took up position N. & S. of hot fire. German H.E. gun fired on horses lines & killed 2 & all killed horses	Killed Gunner McLeod
25-9	In morning German H.E. guns shelled in PARGNAN Ridge & fired in Ecurie Ferme during day into our lines. Horses were removed; during the night the 2 damaged guns at Paissy were removed & brought into trench. O. Battery lines moved further South to men for safety.	
from 26-9 to 14-10	Forces were on this battery moved S.W. to LUPEIGNE the battery shed were on less guard time, though enemy station was shelled occasionally & 1 gun rather badly damaged on the buffer & belt splinters	
14-15/Oct	Battery moved S.W. to LUPEIGNE & entrained at PERFEN THEREMOIS for HAZEBROUCK where batery detrained Oct 21st/Oct	
21st/Oct	Marched to POPERINGHE & billeted	Lieut J.W. Brown gazetted
22nd	Marched to PILKUM & came into action. did not open fire. billeted	21st as posts K.25/15 R.F.A. Gunner Osborn =
23rd	Remained in trenches. billeted	billetted

1st Division
26th Bde. R.F.A.

WAR   DIARY

117th Battery R. F. A.

October

1914

WAR DIARY or INTELLIGENCE SUMMARY

Army Form C. 2118.

Place	Date	Hour	Summary of Events and Information	Remarks and references to Appendices
	26.9.16	14.10.	From now on till Battery SW to LUPEIGNE the Battery spent men on leave guarding Quarry Station two shelled occasionally & 1 gun under haulage on the buffer by shell splinters	
	14/15 Oct		B.B. Coy moved SW to LUPEIGNE and entrained at FERE-EN-TARDENOIS for HAZEBROUCK where Batty billeted till 21st Oct.	
	21st Oct		Marched to MORBECQUE & billeted	
	22nd		Marched to PRADELLES and came into action, but not open fire. Billeted.	Sergt. J.W. Buckton Gunners Operators 2/Lt Grant 2.5.13 Hope Amm. Column
	23		Remained in Reserve billets	

Army Form C. 2118.

WAR DIARY
or
INTELLIGENCE SUMMARY.
(Erase heading not required.)

Instructions regarding War Diaries and Intelligence Summaries are contained in F.S. Regs., Part II. and the Staff Manual respectively. Title pages will be prepared in manuscript.

Hour, Date, Place	Summary of Events and Information	Remarks and references to Appendices
24th Oct.	In morning came into action near PILKEN village & fired on enemy's trenches. Fired 1500 rounds.	
25th	Comparatively quiet day, in the evening relieved by French & concentrated in PILKEN village (a natural place to concentrate, as the village had been well "Black Maria'd" the day before.) While being relieved Germans made strong attack — battery opened fire on the trenches & was reported to have done great damage — Battery marched via N. of YPRES to ZILLEBEKE & billeted. At night 28th Battery marched with 1st Division to VELDHOEK & came into action S. of GHELUVELD. Enfiladed by German battery & lost Q.M.'S waggon — moved position, while moving heavily shelled by German	Wounded @ 2/Lt Coleman
26th	O.F. got into Cul-de-sac; 1 man on waggons hit but probably no casualties. Took up new position about 500 yds S. of GHELUVELD road.	
27th	Fired at enemy's trenches near BECELAERE.	
28th	Unsuccessful: chase shrapnel burst & wounded 2 men	Wounded F. Wern & L/Cpl O. Honey
29th 30th	attack by Germans at dawn — enemy repulsed. Shelled in evening by H.E. Lt Welch killed.	Killed Lt Welch Lt Mansfield G. Fearn

Forms/C. 2118/10.

WAR DIARY
or
INTELLIGENCE SUMMARY.
(Erase heading not required.)

Army Form C. 2118.

Hour, Date, Place	Summary of Events and Information	Remarks and references to Appendices
31st Oct.	Quiet morning. Infantry in front heavily shelled by explosive fire about 3 p.m. Battery was heavily shelled from all sides, but ready from the rear - German attack, extreme Infantry fired great numbers of rounds at short range of German infantry being a man's upkeep of GHELUVELD road. The battery was ordered to withdraw, as the German had broken through in the night. This 4 guns was got away & 2 wagons - 2 wagons lost as the abandoned - No last 2 guns were fired at by German Infantry who had reached the battery wagon position; 3 horses were shot & the gun materials, but the gunners being pushed back in the evening were recovered - The battery suffered any casualties, the shell fire being very heavy - Battery retreated to "HOOGE" & came into action. Took up new position N of HOOGE	Killed Sgt Bradley Wounded D.S.M. Walker Jr Boyle Sgt Graham S. Smith Bouldie Gr Hartley Elliot Ames Strano Fox Ewing Vaughan (W) Jackson Smith Dr Elkington
1st Nov	Day in many marched to position 2 miles S. W. of the 0.G.E. & remained there till evening 1.S.E. were not shelled but were close up to Infantry firing line - Germans attacked every night.	
5th Nov	Moved to HAZEBROUCK to refit.	

1st Division
26th Bde. R.F.A.

WAR DIARY

117th Battery R. F. A.

November

1914

1914

1st Nov.

117 Bty RFA

Early in morning marched to
Fontain 2 miles S. of HOUSE
then until morning of 3rd. Were not
shelled but were close to Infantry
firing line. Germans attacking along
Ordered to HAZEBROUCK to refit

3rd Nov.

117 A Batt, 26th Div
R.F.A.

War Diary

Hour, Date & Place	Summary of Events & Information	Remarks
5–11 Nov.	Relief in HASEBROUCK. Could not report as further troops + train in hut camp.	
12 Nov	Marched through YPRES at VLAERTINGHE.	2Lt C.W. ALLFREY joined
13 Nov	Took over pn of 115 RFA Stations near HOOGE.	
14 "	Shelled out 6 pm by accurate fire of 11.cmph Howitzers.	
15 "	Occupied area for Gun up trenches S. by night. Shot in support all day aviation — too wet for aeroplanes. Mud bad.	
16	Had G break up Infantry attack at 6 by rapid fire. In view of enemy balloon aeroplane. Therefore again under accurate 11 inch Howitzer fire. Tactical situation alarming. Withdrew Machines temporarily. Charge as fm 300° E + occupied residual carrier ground, whence fired on fine to releived by French m 20.15 mustered effort. Snow rid later. Silenced one mortar, broke up an infantry massing. Have shelled wood + trees slew persistently.	Gr Oney wounded
20th		

96

21st. marched in storm 20th billets at near BOERE 4m E TYNNBYTSROVE. Road all night every day 6-3pm. Roads blocked by snow columns, ice so slippery in billets, started 6- ngt. Gt snow fact.

22 up 6.30 am Remained in billets. Regained 27 Re- reinforcements joined on 30th.

1ST DIVISION

26TH BRIGADE R.F.A.

WAR DIARY

JAN - DEC 1915

121/4194

18th Division

26th Brigade R.F.A.

Vol VI. 1 – 31.1.15

26th Bde. R.F.A.

Army Form C. 2118.

WAR DIARY
or
INTELLIGENCE SUMMARY.
(Erase heading not required.)

Instructions regarding War Diaries and Intelligence Summaries are contained in F.S. Regs., Part II. and the Staff Manual respectively. Title pages will be prepared in manuscript.

Hour, Date, Place	Summary of Events and Information	Remarks and references to Appendices
1.1.15.	118 Battery in action 4.30 pm 5 min artillery bombardment. 24th Bde gas and searchlight on German Canal F. of GUINCHY 26 to 32. HQ moved to W18 to app. 1st Bde. HD.	Ref. map MERVILLE - LA BASSÉE
2.1.15.	117 Battery in reserve for 12. Holiday silenced machine gun during morning.	Ref. map FRANCE (BETHUNE) 1:40,000
3.1.15.	116 in reserve. 117 shelled white house in their zone at request of infantry to silence trench mortars.	
4.1.15.	117 Battery fired at enemy reported massing in front of London British at 3 at, at 12 midday in reserve. Major Langstaff took over 117 Battery.	
5.1.15.	116 in reserve. 117 & 118 fired a few rounds in their zone in support of 91st Bde.	
6.1.15.	117 in reserve. 118 in [?] Gave Motherwell 115 W of Their in front of GIVENCHY and	
7.1.15.	116 and 117 N at 1.15 In alternate days 117 silenced 2 machine guns.	
8.1.15.	116 in reserve. 117 & 118 fired at enemy triangulation in their zone. Major R. Hudson slightly wounded.	Major Winship left R.H. for R.H.A. Capt. Marwood posted to 117 Battery
9.1.15.	Artillery bombardment at 12.45 pm. Half spasmodic firing 2.40 117 in reserve at 1pm. Artillery bombardment at 1.25 pm. 116 took up fire 12o pm. 116 in reserve 2.15.	
10.1.15.	Artillery bombardment opened fire against hostile trenches. Heavy bombardment at 1.30 to 2pm. Ld. Capston machine gun at 11am.	
11.1.15.	116 in reserve Battery fired some rounds	Major Hudson returned to 118 Lt. A.P. Flukes killed whilst with infantry
12.1.15.	Major Langstaff posted to 1st Battery 116 in reserve other batteries	
13.1.15.	118 AM relieved by 2nd Of N.D. German bombardment 3pm. Fired on Canal situation.	
14.1.15.	116 Battery in reserve, 117 D 118 fired a fireworks in their zone	
15.1.15.	117 Battery in reserve, quiet day	Lt. Seaman posted to 117 to replace Lt. Matt. Caldwell posted to R.H.A.
16.1.15.	117 Battery in reserve, quiet day.	Major Ruston attached 26 Bde RFA.

26th M RFA

WAR DIARY
or
INTELLIGENCE SUMMARY
(Erase heading not required.)

Army Form C. 2118.

Hour, Date, Place	Summary of Events and Information	Remarks and references to Appendices
17.1.15	26th 18th A.D. & 3rd Bde of RFA moved to F.10 a just N. of Canal. 116 to Reserve	Ref. Map FRANCE (BETHUNE) 1:40,000
18.1.15	Capt. Ellis posted to 116. his Capt Lawrens. 119 to Reserve at OBLINGHAM and 1 Sect. in to 116 & 117 to Reserve at OBLINGHAM. 116 took over 118 2nd 117 a name as before.	
19.1.15	Quiet day. 117 fired at ludek Ho. 3 direct hits. Major Rutter took Command of 117. 3 rounds for gun fired	
20.1.15		
21.1.15		
22.1.15	Quiet days.	
23.1.15	Battery to report.	
24.1.15		
25.1.15	Germans delivered a heavy attack at 7.30 am against section H.3.15. Battour. it was opposed a heavy fire and rept up a slow rate of fire most of the day and night. The 3rd bgf Rn-, 8 several observing officers reported great damage done by our guns and were able to hold them pinned in Cafs as nothing including firmans about 500, no casualties about 100. Congratulations sent by Div for fine shoot to all concerned in this fight. D.117 G.in-Lebt O.C. the Major. have received 1/4 with 13 Nth replaced by 2nd Bde. 116 nearly 16 shells on to 9.2 hy 04. 3 mm shelled them fire the hardest. Bombardments at 8.20, 11.45 am and 1.45 5.30pm Infantry and found dummy officers. repot good fire effect on Enemy.	110 Battery and Station B 116 and 117 B.S. were brought up into reserve just W. of BEUVRY
26.1.15	116 fired at out lost tin 10am, 2 hr Seek batteries hopt up slow rate of fire meanwhile & night and found German reported manning trenches but no attack made.	
27.1.15		
28.1.15	2.Bn.2h 116 fired to support 2nd hy MM who attacked to try & regain lost ground from the 23rd situation. Battries, co-operated with infantry in the zone.	Capt Ellis heck to 25 & 16th & Duty as Orderly Officer
29.1.15	Quiet day. German reported massing but no attack made.	
30.1.15	Quiet day.	
31.1.15		

1st Division

26th Bde. D + H.

Vol VII 1 – 28. 2. 15

Army Form C. 2118.

WAR DIARY 2°/1st B.ac. R.F.A.

or

INTELLIGENCE SUMMARY.

(Erase heading not required.)

Hour, Date, Place	Summary of Events and Information	Remarks and references to Appendices
GIVENCHY 1.2.15	Quiet day. Nothing to report.	2/Lt Allfrey to R.H.A
2.2.15	Quiet.	
3.2.15	6th Inf Bde relieved 3rd Bde. 118th Battery posted to 28th Divn	(118th Battery & 1 S/gbr supply from A.C. left for 28th Divn
4.2.15	Quiet. Feeble attack about 7.15pm. Batteries opened fire & attack was easily beaten off.	
5.2.15	Quiet. A few rounds fired at enemy trenches	2/Lt J.T. Philipson to RHA
6.2.15	116 firing along footpath & W. of Triangle in support of 4 G Batt. attack on Brickstacks. Attack successful. Batteries conld. steady fire on ground beyond. The infantry were able to entrench in the open.	
7.2.15	Enemy attempted to counter attack about 5pm but were beaten off by artillery fire.	H.Q. & Section joined from base
8.2.15	Quiet.	
8.2.15 / 9.2.15	Quiet. Relieved by 31st Bde R.F.A. 2 Sections of Red Battery relieved at dawn on 8.2.15, remaining section stayed in action till dawn 9.2.15. Brigade marched to rest billets about KILLERS	2/Lt H.B. Heath, 2/Lt C.R. Parker joined from Base on 12.2.15
9.2.15 – 28.2.15	Refitting	

C.R. Huyshe
Lt Col R.F.A
(?) 26th Feb 1915

101/4/917

1st Division

26th Bde R.F.A.

Vol VIII 1 — 31.3.15

AW
1896

WAR DIARY 26th Bde RFA

Army Form C. 2118.

INTELLIGENCE SUMMARY
(Erase heading not required.)

Hour, Date, Place	Summary of Events and Information	Remarks and references to Appendices
LILLERS 1.3.15	2 officers per battery went up to LE TOURET to obtain 3rd Bde R.F.A. Battery positions in 64th Battery position by 5pm. Digging position we reconnoitred for 115th RFA (attached) from 25th Bde & Hors. Bde attack from 4th Bde 2nd Div.	Ref Maps BETHUNE 1/40000 sq. naned
LE TOURET 2.3.15 maps	All batteries in action by 6.30 a.m. Registering zones all day. Front covered by 1st Bde from bottom of S.21.C to S.9.d. Zones of batteries 116 Road junction in S.26.a. to width of S.21. Bde HQ & Observations 117 Middle of S.21 to S.15.c.5.5. at Rue St Bois and Rue 115 S.15.c.5.5. to bottom of S.9.d. de CAILLOUR 60 Covering the front 1 section of both. battles 16 for E of GIVENCHY.	115. W. of road in X.17.a 116. junc N of & in Rue de l'Epinette 117. X.17.b. E. of road in X.11.a X.11.b. 60. in X.17.c.0.4. S. of stream LA LOUANNE.
3.3.15	Orders If. O.C. 39 Inf Bde. Registration continued. Enemy's redoubt knocked about by 117. Prepared during the night	
4.3.15	Quiet. Enemy reported to have removed wire entanglements in front of their trenches in several places. Attack expected along the Rue du	
5.3.15	CAILLOUR. Dispositions made to meet it. No attack.	
6.3.15	Quiet in the morning. German trenches on our front bombarded from 2.45 - 3.45 pm. 1/variant French Counter attack at Notredame de LORRETTE. Bombardment continued up at 11pm 7am 7.3.15 German Starshell in use during the night	
7.3.15	Quiet. Looting party dispersed	
8.3.15	60th Battery firing under orders of 2nd Div Arty 11.3.15.	
9.3.15	Engaged enemy battery in S.21.D. Enemy Brentwood Bn 23rd Bde bombarded	
10.3.15	1st Army offensive. Enemy trenches bombarded from 7.30 am till 8.10 am. Burst of fire continued throughout the day.	

Army Form C. 2118.

WAR DIARY
or
INTELLIGENCE SUMMARY.
(Erase heading not required.)

Instructions regarding War Diaries and Intelligence Summaries are contained in F.S. Regs., Part II. and the Staff Manual respectively. Title pages will be prepared in manuscript.

Hour, Date, Place	Summary of Events and Information	Remarks and references to Appendices
LE TOURET 11.3.'15	Offensive continued. Burst of fire on enemy's trenches throughout the day. Infantry on our front quiet. Our observing stations shelled at intervals.	Ref. Map. BETHUNE 1/4000 3 yards
12.3.15	Enemy probable observing stations in Rue D'Ouvert shelled. Fire from enemy artillery considerably increased. Rue du Bois heavily shelled. 114 Battery came into action in S.8.a. about 11 p.m.	
13.3.15	114 Battery registering with a view to cutting wire entanglements. 116 engaged enemy battery in S.29.a. Bursts of fire on enemy's trenches from 4.30 p.m. till 6.30 p.m.	114 ordered not to fire except in case of attack.
14.3.15.	117 silenced hostile mortar in S.15.d. Quiet.	
15.3.15	Billets in RUE DE L'ÉPINETTE shelled. Enemy parapets strengthened and improved.	
16.3.15.	Our billets shelled. 116 & 117 fired bursts at enemy billets in RUE DE MARAIS.	
17.3.15.	114 rejoined 25th Bde. 3 nieb a few rounds on enemy billets. Quiet.	
18.3.15		
19.3.15.	No rounds fired.	
20.3.15	Burst of fire on enemy's trenches to help French advance at NOTRE DAME DE LORETTE. Quiet.	
21.3.15	Quiet	
22.3.15	Burst of fire at 1 a.m this morning as on 20.3.'15.	
23.3.15	115th Bty registered communication trench. All quiet.	
RICHEBOURG 24.3.15	Our positions taken over by the 25th Bde. 26th Bde in action at S.8.6.9.8.} Both batteries in dawn as follows:— 116th Bty in S.8.6.9.8.} observation 117 Bty in S.2.d.3.1.} Reproduction Complete	Positions covering LA BASSÉE road to await 29 Division in S.5 & 11 if required

Army Form C. 2118.

WAR DIARY
or
INTELLIGENCE SUMMARY
(Erase heading not required.)

Instructions regarding War Diaries and Intelligence Summaries are contained in F. S. Regs., Part II. and the Staff Manual respectively. Title pages will be prepared in manuscript.

Hour, Date, Place	Summary of Events and Information	Remarks and references to Appendices
RICHEBOURG		Ref. Maj. BETHUNE ↓
25.3.15	All Quiet. Alternative Observation posts for blocks in Rue du Bois & Avenue Campbell	Savoie
26.3.15	Quiet.	2.3.15 Maj. C.M.C. RUDKIN posted to England
27.3.15	Quiet.	2Lt R.H. LURBOCK posted to Amm Col
28.3.15	All quiet	
29.3.15	117 Registered trenches from West edge of Bois du BIEZ to road running N.W. from La Russie. Quiet.	
30.3.15	Quiet.	2Lt R.E.T. WINDOVER to Trench Mortar Course. 30.3.15
31.3.15	Quiet. Enemy's medium howitzers registered our trenches.	2Lt R.H. LURBOCK attached 116 Bty. 31.3.15

C.S. Murphy
Lt. Col.
O.C. 26 F⸺R.F.A.

121/5256

1st Division

26th Bde. R.F.A.
Vol IX 1 — 30.4.15.

Army Form C. 2118.

WAR DIARY
or
INTELLIGENCE SUMMARY.
(Erase heading not required.)

Instructions regarding War Diaries and Intelligence Summaries are contained in F. S. Regs., Part II. and the Staff Manual respectively. Title pages will be prepared in manuscript.

Hour, Date, Place		Summary of Events and Information	Remarks and references to Appendices
RICHEBOURG	1.4.15	Infantry fired bursts of fire for 10 mins commencing at 4.30 am. At 4.40 am. batteries fired 3 rounds at gas junctions in rear of enemy's trenches from 6 am to 7.30 am. Batteries fired 7 salvos at same target on from Bty has opened fire PORT ARTHUR shelled by heavy shrar	Reference map BETHUNE 1/40,000 Squared
	2.4.15	Quiet.	2/Lt R.H. LUBBOCK posted to 116 Bty 3.4.15
	3.4.15	Quiet.	Maj H. YOUNG posted to 117 Bty 4.4.15
	4.4.15	Quiet. German Balloon seen at S. of La Bassée	
	5.4.15	Quiet.	
	6.4.15	Quiet.	
	7.4.15	Quiet.	
	8.4.15	Quiet.	
	9.4.15	Quiet.	
	10.4.15	Quiet.	
	11.4.15	Quiet.	
	12.4.15	Registered German trenches. Quiet	
	13.4.15	Quiet. 116 covering front of 6th WYM BDE till 12 noon 13/4/15.	
	14.4.15	116 Registered German trenches. Quiet	
	15.4.15	Quiet 116 + 117 in reserve from 12 noon but ready to fire on S.15	
	16.4.15	Positions astride L'Arée South	
	17.4.15	Quiet.	

Army Form C. 2118.

WAR DIARY
or
INTELLIGENCE SUMMARY.
(Erase heading not required.)

Instructions regarding War Diaries and Intelligence Summaries are contained in F. S. Regs., Part II. and the Staff Manual respectively. Title pages will be prepared in manuscript.

Hour, Date, Place	Summary of Events and Information	Remarks and references to Appendices
RICHBOURG 18.4.'15	Batteries registered WHITE HOUSE, DOUBLE HOUSE and trenches in S.15. Quiet.	Reference Map - BETHUNE 1/40,000 Squared.
19.4.15	Quiet.	
20.4.15	Quiet. German aeroplanes active in evening.	
21.4.15	Quiet.	2Lt R.F.T. Windover posted to Trench Mortar Bty.
22.4.'15	Fired with aeroplane observation. Both batteries fired at S.16.c.8.2. and S.21.d. Quiet.	
23.4.15	Quiet	2/Lt O'M.C. Creagh posted 117 Bty 23.4.15 2Lt Q.L. Gordon posted to Amm. Col. 24.4.15.
24.4.'15	Quiet	
25.4.'15	116. Registered trenches in S.15.a. Quiet	
26.4.'15	Quiet	
27.4.15	Quiet	
28.4.15	Quiet	
29.4.15	Quiet	
30.4.15	Quiet.	

G.B. Mingham
Lt. Col.
A/S 26th Bde. R.F.A.

121/5332

1st Division

26th Bde. R. F. A.

1 — 31.5.15

Army Form C. 2118.

WAR DIARY
or
INTELLIGENCE SUMMARY.
(Erase heading not required.)

Instructions regarding War Diaries and Intelligence Summaries are contained in F. S. Regs., Part II. and the Staff Manual respectively. Title pages will be prepared in manuscript.

Hour, Date, Place	Summary of Events and Information	Remarks and references to Appendices
RICHEBOURG		REF: MAP. BETHUNE 40,000 (squared)
1.5.15	Quiet	Pte. J.C.S.W. BARKER wounded 3.5.15
2.5.15	Quiet	Lt. F.Y. BRIGHT attached 116 Bty.} 4.5.15
3.5.15	Quiet	Lt. E.N. O'NEILL attached 117 Bty.}
4.5.15	Quiet	Maj. G.L. POPHAM posted 116 Bty. 5.5.15
5.5.15	Quiet	
6.5.15	Quiet	
7.5.15	Quiet	
8.5.15	Quiet	
4.45-4.52am 9.5.15	Fired registration on German wire & fire to batteries	
5am - 5.10am	Deliberate wire cutting half of fire Battery fire 7 secs	Round flew cutting, 2nd to 3rd top cut gap of 60 yards in S.P.? which were widened later
5.20am - 5.30am	wire cutting continued	
5.30am - 5.40am	Intense bombardment B.? 4 secs. from 5.30am - 5.35am H.E. fired on German parapet	
5.40am	Fire lifted on to German rear trench Advancing in the big Assault. Assault of 25th Bde RFA unsuccessful	Casualties Lt Col G.P.B. Hinton slightly wounded (at Battery)
6.30am - 6.48 am	Fire on German front trench in S.P.A.	
6.48 am - 7pm	Bombardment of German entrenchments to stop enemy supporting Infantry withdrawn covered by fire of the guns	1 OR wounded
7am - 3.20pm	Battery fire to make to order fire on wire	Brigade fired about 2700 rounds
3.20pm - 4.30pm	Bombardment as before Assault unsuccessful	
	Quiet night.	

WAR DIARY
or
INTELLIGENCE SUMMARY.
(Erase heading not required.)

Army Form C. 2118.

Hour, Date, Place	Summary of Events and Information	Remarks and references to Appendices
RICHEBOURG 10.5.15	Quiet	Reference Map:- BETHUNE 40000 Squared. 12/7/15.
11.5.15	Quiet	
12.5.15	Quiet	
13.5.15	Deliberate bombardment starting at dawn and continuing throughout the day and night. 100 rds per gun allowed.	
14.5.'15	15.a.m. - 1.7.a.m. bombardment 4 rds per gun per minute. 3.a.m. batteries withdrawn to billets at LE TOURET	
15.5.15	WILLOE Moved to VERMELLES	
VERMELLES 16.5.15	Batteries in action at dawn. 116 Bty at G.13.b.28. covering front of 1st Bde. 117 Bty at G.13.b.28. covering front of 1st Bde. from roads running N.E. through A.28 inclusive to road running East through G.16. Both batteries registered trenches and roads in rear. Observing stations 116 Bty at Fosse No 3 ; 117 Bty at Fosse No 4.	116 Bty's Zone from road running N.E. through A.28 to dividing line between Q.11 and G.5 117 remainder.
17.5.15	117 Bty took over French position at G.8.d.55. same Zone. Registration continues.	
18.5.15	Four guns 117 and 4 guns 116 registered.	
19.5.15	Section of 116 Bty moves into French position G.8.d.9.9. 6.a.m. registration at dawn.	

Army Form C. 2118.

WAR DIARY
or
INTELLIGENCE SUMMARY.
(Erase heading not required.)

Ref: BETHUNE 40,000 sq.m.

Hour, Date, Place	Summary of Events and Information	Remarks and references to Appendices
VERMELLES. 20.5.'15 7. p.m.	Remaining 2 guns of 116 moved into new position by dawn. Four guns of 46 in action at G.8.C.35 by 6 p.m. and started Registration. 117 Battery registered crossroads H.7.C.44 which were bombarded from 9 p.m. to 10 p.m. (30 rds). 51st Battery moved into action at L.6.a.26. after 9 p.m.	46 Bty & 51st Bty of 39 Bde. tactically placed under Lt. Col G.B. Hunter 20 9/15. Lt. F. Y. BRIGHT & 2/Lt E.N. O'NEILL returned to own unit 20 5/15.
9 p.m - 10 p.m.		
21.5.'15	Remainder of 46 Bty moved into position at dawn and registered. 46 Bty zone between G.5d - G.6.c. and cross roads in G.17d.55. inclusive. 51st Battery registered its zone between VERMELLES-AUCHY road in A.28.b. and Cross roads in G.11d inclusive. 46 Bty and 117 Bty bombarded Cross roads G.6.C.	
7.30 p.m. - 8.30 p.m.	and H.7.C.44 from 7.30 p.m to 8.30 p.m. and occasional rounds during night 21/22 (30 rds per battery.)	
22.5.15	51st Registered. German fire on our trenches returned and occasional rounds fired during night. Quiet day.	Rt. H. GARDNER to hospital 22.5.15.
23.5.15	Continued registration. 117 fired on cross roads G.7.C. where movement was reported.	
24.5.15	Quiet. German KITE seen in direction of HULLOCH	
25.5.15	Quiet.	

Army Form C. 2118.

WAR DIARY
or
INTELLIGENCE SUMMARY.
(Erase heading not required.)

Instructions regarding War Diaries and Intelligence Summaries are contained in F. S. Regs., Part II. and the Staff Manual respectively. Title pages will be prepared in manuscript.

Hour, Date, Place		Summary of Events and Information	Remarks and references to Appendices
VERMELLES	26.5.'15	51st Bty. registered hostile Batteries near FOSSE No 8 and FERME LES BRIQUES and slain their silenced the former. Remainder - retaliation only	REF MAP :- BETHUNE (Squared) 40,000
	27.5.'15	51st Battery registered hostile gun positions. Quiet day.	
	28.5.'15	Quiet.	
	29.5.'15	51st Battery under orders of Col. Carey 39th Bde. 113rd Battery (25 Bde.) placed under orders of Lt. Col. G.R. Sinton, 26th Bde; Battery Zone as before 113 Battery position G.8.a.2.3. and Zone from VERMELLES - AUCHY road (through G.28.C+b) to VERMELLES-CUINCHY road at the Z of Les Briques inclusion. Quiet.	Capt. R.D. Harrison returned to 26th Bde. Amm Col 29.5.15
	30.5.15	Quiet.	
	31.5.15	German aeroplanes active during the day. One section of 116 and one section from 117 moved to new cutting positions after dusk at A.20.a.2.7 and 117 at A.14.c.3.5 both covering front between CAMBRIN - LA BASSÉE main road and the BETHUNE - LA BASSÉE canal	

C. Smith
Lt. Col. R.F.A.
Comdg 26th Bde. R.F.A.

12/5931

1st Division

26th Bde R+R.

Vol XL 1 – 30.6.15.

Army Form C. 2118.

WAR DIARY
or
INTELLIGENCE SUMMARY.
(Erase heading not required.)

Instructions regarding War Diaries and Intelligence Summaries are contained in F. S. Regs., Part II. and the Staff Manual respectively. Title pages will be prepared in manuscript.

Hour, Date, Place		Summary of Events and Information	Remarks and references to Appendices
VERMELLES COINCY	1.6.15	117 heavily shelled by 6 inch Howitzer during the afternoon. Another Austrian Section of 116 and 117 moved to new position after dusk. Section "Y" handed over to 6th London at 8 p.m. After which Bde H.Q. was at F.24.C.27. 9 tactically under the orders of Col. Carey 39th Bde R.3.A.	Ref. BETHUNE 40000 squared Major J C REA attached to 117 Battery 1.6.15
	2.6.15	Remaining sections of 116 + 117 in action after dusk.	
	3.6.15	Waggon lines in BETHENVILLE WOOD. F16. shelled. Observing Stations - 116 in house A20.b.6.1. and 117 in houses at A.15.C.1.4. and A15C.86.	1 O.R. wounded
	4.6.15	Ranges on enemy's trenches.	
	5.6.15	Quiet	
	6.6.15	117 Registered HOHENZOLLERN FORT in G.4.b.	
	7.6.15	Quiet	
	8.6.15	Registration of trenches Quiet in zone. Quiet	
	9.6.15	Quiet	11/6/15 Capt R.D. HARRISON posted to 118 Capt G. DEAN posted to 26th Bde Amm. Col.
	10.6.15	Quiet	
	11.6.15	Quiet	
	12.6.15	Quiet	
	13.6.15	Feeling for wire by both batteries	
	14.6.15	Few rounds fired on wire	

WAR DIARY
or
INTELLIGENCE SUMMARY.
(Erase heading not required.)

Army Form C. 2118.

Instructions regarding War Diaries and Intelligence Summaries are contained in F.S. Regs., Part II. and the Staff Manual respectively. Title pages will be prepared in manuscript.

Hour, Date, Place		Summary of Events and Information	Remarks and references to Appendices
COINCHY.	15.6.15	Quiet	Ref = BETHUNE. 40,000 (square)
	16.6.15	Waggon lines in F.16.d shelled during day and night of 17.6.15	
	17.6.15	Batteries registered, some enemy 2nd & 3rd line trenches. Quiet.	
	18.6.15	116 Bty shelled by field guns.	1.O.R Killed 18.6.15
	19.6.15	Ordered to move at 12.30 a.m. to bivouac in E.10 & 37. Completed by 6.30 a.m. Amm Col remained in its position at F.18.6.8.0. Bde under orders to move at one hours notice.	2/Lt A. Empson posted to 116 Bty Capt R.D. Harrison joined 116 Bty. 18.6.15
ANNEZIN	20.6.15	Rest. Amm. Col. joined up by 6.30 p.m.	
	21.6.15	Rest. Under four hours notice to move. Exercises carried out only.	Lt J.W. Littleton to hospital 21.6.15
	22.6.15	Rest	Maj. G.B. Oliver to England on promotion 22.6.15
	23.6.15	Rest	
FERFAY.	24.6.15	Moved at 2 p.m. with Division to rest billets in FERFAY. Arrived 6 p.m.	Ref= FRANCE Sheet 36 1/40,000 (square)
	25.6.15	Rest. Still under orders to move at 4 hours notice.	
	26.6.15	Rest.	
	27.6.15	Rest.	
	28.6.15	Rest.	
VERMELLES	29.6.15	Brigade moves to relieve 31 Bde RFA in Section "Y" at 2 p.m. In action at VERMELLES by 11 p.m. 40 (How) Battery 43rd Bde and 15 London Bty (T.F.) attached to 26th Bde. Battery positions: 116 Bty G.7.d.9.1; 117 Bty G.8.c.17.3; 40 Hows. G.8.c.17.3; 15 London T.F G.8.a.0.7	2 Lt C.V. Cumming posted to Amm Col. 2 Lt G.L. Easton posted to 116 Bty. 2 Lt H.S. Brown and 2/Lt G.W. Walker attached 117 Bty 2 Lt C.T. Ranken attached 115 Bty Dated 29.6.15

Army Form C. 2118.

WAR DIARY
or
INTELLIGENCE SUMMARY.
(Erase heading not required.)

Instructions regarding War Diaries and Intelligence Summaries are contained in F. S. Regs., Part II. and the Staff Manual respectively. Title pages will be prepared in manuscript.

Hour, Date, Place	Summary of Events and Information	Remarks and references to Appendices
VERMELLES. 29.6.15 (cont.)	Arcs of fire:- 116. South through centre G.23 North VERMELLES- HULLUCH road inclusive. 117. -"- VERMELLES- HULLUCH Rd inclusive North, FORT HOHENZOLLERN (G.4.b) inclusive. 40. -"- VERMELLES- HULLUCH Rd exclusive -"- Trough 2 of Les Briques 15 (T.F) -,- York road G.12.a.56 North Branch of railway at G.3.b Waggon lines in LABOURSE	REF:- BETHUNE 1/40,000 Square 2nd Edition.
30.6.15.	Registration 116 & 117 completed	

C.S.T… Lt Col RFA
OC 2 Bde RFA

121/6326

1st 15 Division

26th No. Bde R+H.
Vol XII

1-31-4-15

Army Form C. 2118.

WAR DIARY
or
INTELLIGENCE SUMMARY.
(Erase heading not required.)

Instructions regarding War Diaries and Intelligence Summaries are contained in F. S. Regs., Part II. and the Staff Manual respectively. Title pages will be prepared in manuscript.

Hour, Date, Place	Summary of Events and Information	Remarks and references to Appendices
VERMELLES		REF: BETHUNE 1/40,000 2nd Edition
1.7.15	Repairing trenches and replying to enemy's fire.	
2.7.15	Quiet.	
3.7.15	Enemy in answer to enemy shelling VERMELLES. Two guns of 7/5 Mountain Bty, under command of Lt. Col. Fenton, came in place at G.27.c.8.6 firing on "T" section.	
4.7.15	NOYELLES shelled from 12.30 p.m. to 2 p.m. General activity on part of enemy's artillery which was replied to.	
5.7.15	Enemy's artillery still fairly active.	
6.7.15	Burst of fire by enemy's enfilade field howitzer on working party near NOYELLES during day and night. Aeroplane patrol worked with 40E Bty for 3 hours without any apparent result.	
7.7.15	Retaliation only. One gun 15 London withdrawn to waggon line.	Capt A.C. Birch posted to 117 Bty 7.7.15 joined
8.7.15	Retaliation. Section of 113 Bty R.F.A. in position to relieve 15 London and another section at G.32.c.6.4. (GRENAY) to fire on G.17 and G.23 in case of attack only. Both in action by daylight 9.7.15	
9.7.15	NOYELLES shelled intermittently. Remaining section of 113 R.F.A. relieve 15 London after dark.	
10.7.15	Fosse No 3 shelled heavily.	
11.7.15	Quiet. Retaliation only.	
12.7.15	Quiet. Retaliation only.	

Army Form C. 2118.

WAR DIARY
or
INTELLIGENCE SUMMARY.
(Erase heading not required.)

Instructions regarding War Diaries and Intelligence Summaries are contained in F.S. Regs., Part II. and the Staff Manual respectively. Title pages will be prepared in manuscript.

Hour, Date, Place		Summary of Events and Information	Remarks and references to Appendices
VERMELLES	13.7.15	NOYELLES shelled 115 Bty RFA in action at A.6.a.27 Zone from A.27.b.22. to VERMELLES - HULLUCH road and placed under O.C. "Y" Section group (Lt.Col. G.B. Hunter)	Ref. Map :- BETHUNE 20,000
	14.7.15	25th Bde HQ relieved 26th Bde HQ at 10 a.m., batteries remaining in action as before. 26th Bde HQ rest at VERQUINEUL	Capt. A.C. BIRCH posted to 39 Bde RFA 14.7.15 Joined
	15.7.15	Quiet. Relaxation only. HQ resting	
	16.7.15	Ditto	
	17.7.15	Ditto	Maj. A.G. YOUNG posted as Brigade Maj. 1st Div. Arty 17.7.15 Joined
	18.7.15	Ditto	
	19.7.15	Ditto	
	20.7.15	Section of 116 Bty relieved section of 113 Bty at GRENAY. One section of 15 Divl Bty's attached to each battery in "Y" Group for instruction in place of sections taken out to rest. Quiet	
	21.7.15	Quiet	
	22.7.15	Quiet	
	23.7.15	Zones changed. 113 from VERMELLES - HULLUCH road to FORT HOHENZOLLERN exclusive. 116 Bty from VERMELLES - HULLUCH road to VERMELLES - LOOS road both inclusive. 117 Bty same as 116 Bty	inclusive
	24.7.15	Rt Bde HQ relieved 25 Bde HQ in "Y" section by 10 am in NOYELLES. German artillery active firing on village and billets behind firing line	Casualties:- 3.O.R. wounded 24/7
	25.7.15	Quiet. 115 Bty successfully fired on G.6.b with aeroplane observation	
	26.7.15	Quiet. 117 Bty successfully fired on G.13.a.30. with aeroplane	Lt. G.C. KEMP posted as Rm.f. Capt. to 117 Bty. Joined 2/Lt. V.R. HUBBARD attached 116 Rty 26.7.15. R.O.R. wounded

Forms/(C. 2118/10).

WAR DIARY
or
INTELLIGENCE SUMMARY.

(Erase heading not required.)

Army Form C. 2118.

Hour, Date, Place		Summary of Events and Information	Remarks and references to Appendices
VERMELLES	27.7.15	Resolution only	Ref Map :- BETHUNE 1/40,000.
	28.7.15	Villages, NOYELLES, and SAILLY shelled at 5 p.m. otherwise quiet.	Lt. F. WHITEHOUSE (T.F.) att⁰ 116 B⁺ʸ
	29.7.15	Our front and support line heavily shelled about 12.15 p.m. More artillery activity during whole day.	Lt. J. ARMSTRONG att⁰ 117 B⁺ʸ 27.7.15
	30.7.15	Quiet. Resolution only	Capt. the Hon. G.E. BOSCAWEN D.S.O. posted to 116 B⁺ʸ 31.7.15. Ppnces.
	31.7.15	ditto	

C.B. Knight Lt.
Comdg 26th Bde. RFA

121/6753

an a/6

1st 15 wrein

26th Bde R. + A.

Bat XIII

August 15

121/6753

Army Form C. 2118.

WAR DIARY
or
INTELLIGENCE SUMMARY.
(Erase heading not required.)

Instructions regarding War Diaries and Intelligence Summaries are contained in F. S. Regs., Part II. and the Staff Manual respectively. Title pages will be prepared in manuscript.

Hour, Date, Place	Summary of Events and Information	Remarks and references to Appendices
VERMELLES		REF MAP - BETHUNE 40,000
1.8.15	Retaliation only	
2.8.15	NOYELLES and VERMELLES shelled (5.9") at 7 pm otherwise Quiet	
3.8.15	Enemy's working parties dispersed in front of T1 three times during day	MAJ: WILLIAMS attached for instruction and joined 3-8-15. Left 10-8-15.
4.8.15	Quiet	Capt E.B. MAXWELL posted to Army Command of 117 Bty 4.8.15
5.8.15	Quiet. 15 D[i]st sections attached & group finally withdrawn	Lt: J.D.G. MacNEECE posted as O.O[?] 26th Bde R.F.A. 4.8.15.
6.8.15	Quiet	MAJ. R.D. HARRISON proceeded to England on promotion 5.8.15
7.8.15	VERMELLES shelled more heavily than usual	
8.8.15	Quiet. Usual daily shelling took on Bty positions every day. Thick fog.	
9.8.15	Quiet	
10.8.15	Quiet	
11.8.15	Quiet	1st Div[i]s[ion]. Horse shows ANNEZIN
12.8.15	Quiet	
13.8.15	Quiet	
14.8.15	Quiet	
15.8.15	Quiet	
16.8.15	Quiet	
17.8.15	Quiet	
18.8.15	Quiet	
19.8.15	Quiet. Torpadoes made their first appearance in "Y" Group. All Btys fired 2 rds gun fire at 9.30 pm and 10.30 pm in hopes of catching reliefs.	
20.8.15	Quiet.	

Army Form C. 2118.

WAR DIARY
or
INTELLIGENCE SUMMARY
(Erase heading not required.)

Instructions regarding War Diaries and Intelligence Summaries are contained in F. S. Regs., Part II. and the Staff Manual respectively. Title pages will be prepared in manuscript.

Hour, Date, Place	Summary of Events and Information	Remarks and references to Appendices
VERMELLES 21.8.15	H.Q. 26th Bde. handed over "Y" Group to H.Q. 25th Bde. and moved to Verquigneul. Btys. remaining in action as before	Ref: BETHUNE 1/40000
22.8.15	Quiet. Retaliations only, and working	
23.8.15	on Battery positions to obtain the	
24.8.15	necessary 8.ft of cover	
25.8.15		
26.8.15		
27.8.15		
28.8.15		
29.8.15		
30.8.15		
31.8.15		

Maj. R.F.A.
for Lt.-Col. Comdg. 26 H.B. de R.F.A.

WAR DIARY

Headquarters,

26th BRIGADE, R.F.A.

(1st Division)

S E P T E M B E R

1 9 1 5

WAR DIARY or INTELLIGENCE SUMMARY.

(Erase heading not required.)

Army Form C. 2118.

Hour, Date, Place	Summary of Events and Information	Remarks and references to Appendices
VERMELLES. 1.9.15	Quiet. Position of wagon lines moved during night to Noeux-Les-Mines (L.13.a.40) and 26 Amm. Col. to Hesdigneul (K.2.b). Bty. under orders of 22ⁿᵈ Bde R.F.A. to 10 a.m. 3.9.15.	REF MAP : BETHUNE 1/40,000.
2.9.15	Bde. H.Q. moved to Noyelles (L.17.b.28) at 9 a.m. Section of 116 Bty. at Maroc (G.32.c.84) returned to Bty. during night 2⁄3⁄9. 117 Bty. moved to position S. of 116 Bty. (L.13.a.88) night 2⁄3⁄9. Quiet. Retaliation only.	Lt. Ruthven joined 26ᵗʰ Bde R.A.A. and Jones 28.9.15
3.9.15	26ᵗʰ Bde. under orders of "C" Group. 157 Div. from 10 a.m. 3.9.15 and is moved to Vermelles (L.13.a.02). Shoves and to wagon line Noeux.	"C" Group consists of H.Q. Col. Elton. 2ⁿᵈ Machine and L. Fusars and men from 25ᵗʰ & 26ᵗʰ Bdes at H.Q.
4.9.15	Zone = 116 + 117 Btys. Vermelles - Huluch road to Long Tree (G.17.c.91) into melinite. Alternate zone retaliation.	
5.9.15	Quiet.	
6.9.15	Quiet.	
7.9.15	"C" 71 Bty. in action at G.14.a.94 placed under 26ᵗʰ Bde orders. Zones of batteries - 116 Bty. G.11.d.93 (inclusive) to G.17.c.9.3 (inclusive). 117 Bty G.17.c.9.3 (exclusive) to G.22.d.6.6 (inclusive).	"C" Group changes to 1ˢᵗ D.A. Group 26ᵗʰ Bde. becomes a sub group 7⁄9
8.9.15	"C" 71 registering new front. Quiet. New position selected for two gun Bty. (18 pdr) just N. of C.71 Bty. at G.14.6.18. and one 4.5" How Bty. at G.14.a.61.	
9.9.15	Digging gun emplacements for new Btys. 100 men supplied by Inf. to work at night 9⁄10. Quiet.	
10.9.15	Three batteries shot by aeroplane on prominent points behind German front line. C.71 shelled in afternoon by 4.2". Some direct hits on one gun and on 116 O.P. No loss. Work continued on new emplacement.	
11.9.15	Quiet. Work on gun pits continued. C.71 fired by aeroplane. 100 men 10ᵗʰ Gloucesters attached as working party.	2 O.R. wounded 116 Bty. 2 O.R. killed 3 O.R. wounded } C.71 Bty.

Army Form C. 2118.

WAR DIARY
or
INTELLIGENCE SUMMARY.
(Erase heading not required.)

Instructions regarding War Diaries and Intelligence Summaries are contained in F.S. Regs., Part II. and the Staff Manual respectively. Title pages will be prepared in manuscript.

Hour, Date, Place		Summary of Events and Information	Remarks and references to Appendices
VERMELLES	12.9.15	German artillery active all day and fired on working parties during night of 12th/13th. Retaliations carried out. D107 Bty (18pdr) and A109 Bty (4.5" How.) came under orders of 26th Bde Group and one in action by dawn 13.9.15. 26th Bde AC moved to E.28.a.55.	Ref Map. BETHUNE 1/40,000 & TRENCH MAP 36 N.W. 3 + Part of 1/10,000
	13.9.15	Positions of A109 at G.14.a.4.1 and D107 at G.14.a.9.6 (just N. of C.7¹ Bty) 116, 117, & A109 fired by aeroplane. C.107 Bty placed under 26th Bde in morning and normal by dawn 14th and is in action at G.14.a.10.8 (by dawn 14th	
	14.9.15	Batteries formed into two sub-groups. Northern sub group consists of 116, 117, C.71, & A109 and is under 26th Bde, C + D107 being in S. sub group. C.71 & A109 fired by aeroplane. Germans heavily shelled Sap D and annexes (G.17a) heavily shelled all day Sap D and support trenches (G.17a) heavily shelled all day.	2Lt O'MOORE EBBAGH posted to coy for TRENCH MORTAR SCHOOL 15.9.15
	15.9.15	Same as 15.9.15. 116 Bty blew up bomb store & gas cylinders behind BOIS CARRÉ	
	16.9.15		
	17.9.15	Quiet. 116 Bty dispersed working parties	Lt A. BARR R.V.C. reported and rejoined 26th Bde RFA
	18.9.15	Quiet	Lt Rothven AVC posted to 26 Bde RFA
	19.9.15	Quiet. Working parties dispersed	2Lt H. THOMAS, RFA posted to 26 Bde and attached 117 Bty
	20.9.15	Quiet.	2Lt S.A. PAIGE R.F.A. attached 26 Bde A.C. 17.9.15
	21.9.15	2 am 1st Gloucesters working party left. Bombardment of enemy's trenches commenced today were to be cut by Bty as follows:- 116 Bty. Sap head & front wire G.17.a.94. Sap G.17.a.9.4. to G.17.b.6.0 and G.17.b.6.0 to G.17.b.15. 117 Bty. G.11.d.7.3 to G.17.c.8.1. C.71 Bty. G.17.d. [?] 1.5 to G.23.a.10.10 inclusive of wire round sap and sap head G.17.c.8.1.	2Lt V. GUNN RFA attached 116 Bty 13.9.15

WAR DIARY or INTELLIGENCE SUMMARY.

(Erase heading not required.)

Army Form C. 2118

Hour, Date, Place	Summary of Events and Information	Remarks and references to Appendices
VERMELLES		Ref Map :- BETHUNE 1/40,000 and TRENCH MAP 36ᴺᵂ. Nº 3 & part 1. 1/10,000
21.9.15 (cont.)	A109 bombard 2ⁿᵈ line trench. Night lines as wire cutting zone & also zones in case of enemy attack. Very weak German reply.	
22.9.15	Bombardment continued. Demonstration at 7.55am to 8.6am on front line trenches Rue Ouvert successful.	Nº of rds fired by Bty from 21ˢᵗ to 24ᵗʰ inclusive :—
23.9.15	Bombardment continued. Satisfactory wire cutting. Many gaps made. Firing night 23/24 at least 12 rounds each per hour.	H.E. Shrapnel Total 116 Bty 211 2968 3179 117 Bty 571 3245 3816 C/71 Bty 183 1958 2141 A109 1220 shrapnel & 20 shrapnel
24.9.15	Bombardment continued. Little or no German reply. Demonstration at 1.55pm to 2.6pm. Satisfactory gaps in wire widened.	Total 16 guns :— 965 HE + 9171 Shrapnel 20 guns : 10,376
25.9.15.	During night of 24/25 wagon lines moved to 6.1.b.6. and B.A.C. to L.7.c.	Grand total : 10,376
4 a.m.	Bde HQ moved to Fighting Station at G.16.a.8.2. close to 1ˢᵗ Bde.	
5.50 a.m.	Bombardment began as shown on attached time table. O'Bring ordered at 5.50 a.m.	
6.30 a.m.	Infantry attacked; an officer from each battery being with the leading Batts. Patrols successful except S.W. of Bois Carré and in front of 2ⁿᵈ Inf Bde.	
7 a.m.	Bde H.Q. moved with 1ˢᵗ Inf Bde H.Q. to old Black Watch H.Q. at G.17.a.35. Communication with Btys & Group also between F.O.'s and Btys broke down. Orders sent direct to Btys from 1ˢᵗ D.A. Group.	
8.30 a.m.	116 Bty firing on Hulluch.	
11.15 a.m.	116 Bty moves forward to G.15.C.74. S. of LE RUTOIRE and fires on trenches behind LONE TREE	

INTELLIGENCE SUMMARY.

(Erase heading not required.)

Instructions regarding War Diaries and Intelligence Summaries are contained in F.S. Regs., Part II. and the Staff Manual respectively. Title pages will be prepared in manuscript.

Hour, Date, Place	Summary of Events and Information	Remarks and references to Appendices
VERMELLES 26.9.15 cont.		REF MAP:- TRENCH MAP, 36° N.W. 3. AND Part of 1. 1/10,000
11.30 a.m.	Since communication between H.Q. & Btys was still broken O.C. Bde went forward to Bty Comdrs and observed fire with them from 2nd line trenches before that line had been fully taken	
12 midday	117 Bty move forward to position at G.15c78 S. of Le Rotoir.	25.9.15 Casualties:- O.R. Killed. 2.
12.45 pm	116 Bty firing on trenches E. of HULLUCH	Wounded:-
1.30 pm	Bde HQ moved up with 1st Inf Bde HQ to G.11.d.9.3 and thence to G.18.a.76	Lt.Col. G.B. Hinton [slight, still at duty.]
2 pm	Trenches behind LONE TREE shelled by 116 Bty. Shortly afterwards these trenches were surrendered.	Major G.L. Popham 116 Bty. Capt E.B. Maxwell 117 Bty. O.R. 6
2.15 pm	117 Bty moved up into action at G.17.6.20. just N. of HAIE DE BOIS CARRE and began firing on HULLUCH	
3.30 pm	(How) Bty came into action at G.15.c.6.2 just S. of HAIE DE BOIS CARRE under Bde orders and fired into HULLUCH	
4.45 pm	116 Bty shelled PUITS 14 bis and trenches S. of it. During morning 117 Bty was shelled with gas shells which did little damage	
6. pm	After dark Bde HQ moved back to German front line trenches at G.17.6.10 for the night being in telephonic communication with 1st Inf Bde at G.18.a.27	
	NIGHT LINES:-	
	All three batteries on roads & trenches E. of main road H.17.C.52. to H.13.C.A.5 (outer defences of HULLUCH) There was a lad day for observing fire amongst between 12 noon and 3 pm	

Instructions regarding War Diaries and Intelligence Summaries are contained in F. S. Regs., Part II. and the Staff Manual respectively. Title pages will be prepared in manuscript.

INTELLIGENCE SUMMARY.

(Erase heading not required.)

Hour, Date, Place	Summary of Events and Information	Remarks and references to Appendices
26.9.15	HQ in touch with 3rd Inf. Bde. who had taken over from 1st Inf. Bde. Batteries observed fire from G.15.6.35	REF. MAP: TRENCH MAP 36¢ N.W. No 3 + part 5 1/10,000
7.30 a.m.	117 Bty stopped counter-attack during night 25/26	
8. a.m.	30 Bty stopped counter attack S. of HULLUCH	26.9.15
9.30 a.m.	30 Bty Gas shells at intervals from non onwards	CASUALTIES:
	117 Bty stopped counter-attack from HULLUCH causing enemy heavy casualties	Wounded:— Capt C.C. KEMP 117 Bty 2/Lt H.B. HINDLE 117 Bty
10 a.m. — 11 a.m.	Bombardment Inferno from 10.45 a.m. to 11 a.m.	O.R. 6
	116 Bty barraged from H.17.d.5.1 to H.18.c.9.3	
	117 Bty fired on trenches W. of HULLUCH H.13.b.19 - H.13.b.05	POSTINGS:—
	30 Bty outer defences of HULLUCH.	Capt. T.D.G. MACNEECE to take command 116 Bty
11.30 a.m. — 12.noon	Attack delayed till 12 noon. Bombardment as above. After 12 noon whole Bde barraged	Capt. H.N. FAIRBANK from us/staff to temp. command 117 Bty
	H.8.c.9.3 — H.14.c.2.5.	Lt A.B. RUSHER E. ADJUTANT
12. noon	Attack by 3rd Inf Bde successful but owing to Divs on the right failing and retiring, 3rd Bde was forced to return to its original trenches.	Mr E.T. DRISCOLL to 117 Bty
12.30 p.m.	117 Bty shelled by Gas shells which continued at intervals all day. The wagon and a limber completely destroyed at 3 p.m. 3 guns temporarily out of action. Moved back 150" during afternoon	
4. p.m.	30th Bty moved back to G.14 & 6.2 and placed under charge/orders of 1st DA Group	
	NIGHT LINES:— All Btys:—	
	H.13.b.17 — H.13.c.42 — H.13.c.09 — G.13.d.56, Bde HQ, Same as night 25/26	
	and in telephonic communication with 3rd Inf. Bde.	

INTELLIGENCE SUMMARY.

(Erase heading not required.)

Instructions regarding War Diaries and Intelligence Summaries are contained in F.S. Regs., Part II and the Staff Manual respectively. Title pages will be prepared in manuscript.

Hour, Date, Place	Summary of Events and Information	Remarks and references to Appendices
27.9.15 12.30 a.m.	117 Bty moved back to its old position at VERMELLES G.13656 in observation. In action by 4.30 a.m. but did not fire all day. Fairly quiet all the morning	REF MAP - TRENCH MAP 36c N.W. 3 & Part I. 1/10,000
3.30 p.m. to 4.50 p.m.	Bombardment. 116 Bty bombarded German trenches from PUITS 13bis (H140q.3) to H18Q23	27.9.15 CASUALTIES:- 3 O.R. wounded.
4.50 p.m.	Attack on HILL 70 by GUARDS DIVn. Partially successful. Night lines:- 116 Bty PUITS 1360 to KEEP H206 inclusive 117 Bty H13611 to H13617 Rate of fire 24 rds per Bty per hour	
28.9.15	Fairly quiet.	
1 p.m. to 6.30 p.m.	116 Bty formed a barrage on Cross Roads in HULLUCH and trenches E. of it - H12a39 to H14a07 inclusive. 100 rds per Bty per hour. Night lines and night firing on night 27/28.	28.9.15 CASUALTIES:- 1 O.R. wounded POSTINGS:- 2/Lt W.C. MITCHELL to 117 Bty
29.9.15	Quiet. 116 Bty position shelled at intervals all day. 3rd INF BDE relieved during night 29/30 by Guards. Bde H.Q. moved back to old H.Q. at VERMELLES and took temporary charge of 1st D.A. Group batteries consisting of 24th Bty, 85th Bde, 30th (How) Bty and 2nd Siege Bty.	
3 p.m.	Night Lines:- 116 Bty PUITS 136is (H14c) to KEEP H206 inclusive 117 Bty H13611 to H13617. No night firing	
30.9.15	Quiet. 116 Bty position shelled at intervals all day. Change of 1st D.A. Group Btys reverts to 1st D.A. Group. Night lines as 29th. No night firing.	30.9.15 CASUALTIES 1 O.R. wounded

G.H.W. Nunn Lt.Col
Comdg 26th Bde RFA

N.B. The 1st period actually lasted till 1.15. then 2nd Period began

1st DIVISIONAL ARTILLERY GROUP TIME TABLE.

Bde.	Battery.	1rd pr gun per minute 1st Period. 0. - 0.40.	2 rds per gun per min 1st Lift. 0.40 - 0.48.	1 rd per gun per min. 2nd Lift. 0.48 - 1.15
26.	117th.	Front line trenches and Communication trenches running back from front line.	G.18.b.5.10 - G.18.b.90. 3rd line trenches and Communication trenches running back from 3rd line.	H.13.b.1. 7. - H.13.d.2.4.
	116th			
71.	C.	2nd line trenches and Communication trenches running back from 2nd line including trench G.12.c.6.0. - G.12.c. 10.6.	2nd line trenches and Communication trenches running back from 2nd line omitting trenches from .G.18.a.2.3 - G.17.b.8.1. G.18.d.8.8 - G.18.c.1.8. G.17.d.8.8 - G.18.c.1.6. G.12.c.6.0 - G.12.d.10.6.	Barrage along Road from H.13.d.2.4 - H.19.a.8.0.
109.	A. 4.5.	2nd line G.12.d.0.6. to G.17.d.70 and Communication trenches from front line. Second	3rd line G.12.d.70 - G.12.b.3.5 Outer defences of HULLUCH G.18.b.9.2. and Communication and Communication trenches trenches from 2nd line. running back from 3rd line.	2nd line to include G. 18.a.3.2. G.18.c.8.9. P.T.O.

TARGETS for Batteries as under -

1st Period.

116 Bty -: 6 guns front line trenches LONE TREE to SAP 94.
117 Bty -: G.11 d 73 to G.17 b.52.
C71 Bty -: G.12c 6.1. to G.12c 10.5 and
G.18a.2.3 to G.18c.89
A109 -: 1 gun at each of following.
    G.18 a 2.3 & 50ᵡ search
    G.17 d.8.1. & sweep
    G.18 a 7.6 & 50ᵡ search
    G.12.C.6.2 to G.12C.10.5.

2nd Period

116 Bty -: G.18 b. (trenches)
117 Bty -: G.18 b. (— " —)
C71 Bty -: Trench G.18a 23 to G.18 c.89.
A109 Bty -: Comm. Trench G.18a 76 to G.18 b.92

3rd Period.

116 Bty -: H13 b 12 to H13a.24.
117 Bty -: ~~H13b17~~ Trenches round H of HULLUCH.
C71. Bty -: Cross Roads on HULLUCH - LENS road.
A109 Bty -: H 13d (trenches & cross R.)

121/7468

1st Bavarian
26th Bav. R.I.A.

Oct. 16

Vol XV

Army Form C. 2118.

WAR DIARY
or
INTELLIGENCE SUMMARY.
(Erase heading not required.)

Hour, Date, Place	Summary of Events and Information	Remarks and references to Appendices
VERMELLES.		REF: MAP:- TRENCH MAP.
1.10.15.	Waggon Lines of 116 & 117 Batteries moved back to their old positions.	36.c. N.W. 3rd part sheet 1.
	NOEUX LES MINES. L.13.d.	BETHUNE 1:40,000
	Batteries Registering	O.R. Wounded 3.
2.10.15.	Quiet all day	
3.10.15.	Batteries Registering.	
	Both Batteries Zones from PUITS 14 bis to CITÉ ST ELIE.	O.R. Wounded 2.
	116 Battery was shelled in the morning.	
4.10.15.	Quiet all day	
	116 Battery & 117 Battery Zones taken over by Guards Division Batteries at midday, but both Batteries had to be prepared to fire in them during the night	
5.10.15.	117 Battery moved to new position G.14.c.94 during the night	
6.10.15.	116 Battery & 117 Battery covering new Zone Hill c.1.20 to H.13.c.1.1.	Lt. Le Page reported to 25th Bn. at
	Batteries Registering	117 to Dressing at L.23.0.6.7. Nr. RA Schools att. to Buie ae 6/10/15.
		116 to hillside Funne 3 at G.19.b.1.5.

WAR DIARY
or
INTELLIGENCE SUMMARY.

(Erase heading not required.)

Army Form C. 2118.

Hour, Date, Place	Summary of Events and Information	Remarks and references to Appendices
VERMELLES 7.10.15	Quiet all day. 116 Battery & 117 Battery fired 50 rounds per Battery on No Man's Land through the night on their Zones to prevent enemy digging.	REF MAP:- TRENCH MAP. 36 C N W 2nd part of 1 BETHUNE 1/40,000.
8.10.15	Enemy heavily bombarded the front held by 1st Division	
12.30 p.m. to 3 p.m.	H.M.a L.7 & LOOS especially CHALK PITS and CHALK PIT WOOD. Communications behind the line were heavily shelled.	
3. p.m.	Enemy attacked and was replied with heavy losses. Owing to smoke caused by bombardment making observation impossible, 28th Brigade batteries formed a barrage of fire in front of enemy trenches from N.25.L.25 to 36.L.9.15. Telephone communication was kept up throughout the day from 28th Brigade Headquarters to Batteries & from Batteries to Forward Observing Officers. 117 Battery fired at intervals through the night on their Zone. 116 Battery did no night firing but were prepared to open fire in case of an attack	

Army Form C. 2118.

WAR DIARY
or
INTELLIGENCE SUMMARY.
(Erase heading not required.)

Instructions regarding War Diaries and Intelligence Summaries are contained in F.S. Regs., Part II and the Staff Manual respectively. Title pages will be prepared in manuscript.

Hour, Date, Place	Summary of Events and Information	Remarks and references to Appendices
VERMELLES 9.10.15	Quiet all day. 116 Battery fired at intervals through the night in their zone. 117 Battery did one night shoot & has been prepared to open fire in case of an attack.	REF MAP:- TRENCH MAP 36.c. N.W. B[th]part of BETHUNE 1/40,000
10.10.15	116 Battery wire cutting all day. H.13.a.1.2. & H.13.a.4.2.h. Wire thinned. Only H.E. used. 117 Battery did not fire.	
11.10.15	116 Battery wire cutting as before. Several gaps cut. 117 Battery wire cutting H.13.a.4.2.h. & H.13.a.4.1. Wire thinned. N.E. heavy hy fd hit Batteries. Forward position for 4 guns of 117 Battery reconnoitred and chosen at G.17.d.8.2. to G.23.b.2.9.	

Army Form C. 2118.

WAR DIARY
or
INTELLIGENCE SUMMARY.
(Erase heading not required.)

Instructions regarding War Diaries and Intelligence Summaries are contained in F.S. Regs., Part II. and the Staff Manual respectively. Title pages will be prepared in manuscript.

Hour, Date, Place	Summary of Events and Information	Remarks and references to Appendices
VERMELLES		Ref. Map.— TRENCH MAP 36c N.W. 3 & 1 part 1. BETHUNE 1/40,000
12.10.15	Both Batteries went on supplying Saps in wire entanglement	
12.30 p.m. to 2.30 p.m.	116 Battery was heavily shelled. 116 waggon lines were shelled in the afternoon. Communication trenches were made during the day. 117 Battery moved & Guns shifted to a forward position in the open at G.6.17.d.3.2 to G.23.b.2.9	O.R. wounded 4. 2Lt. H.B. Hanson posted to 116 Bty. 12/10/15.
13.10.15	116 Battery wire cutting in the morning with 2 guns in trenches. 117 Battery wire cutting during the morning. 117 Battery & forward guns fired a few rounds for night registration. Both Batteries were in turn attacked. But Batteries formed a barrage of fire in front of infantry which was continued throughout the night. 117 Battery & forward guns very heavily shelled in the afternoon. Communication was seriously disorganised throughout the day.	O.R. died of wounds 1 O.R. wounded 5. Lt. W.F. Mitchell slightly wounded (at duty).

(9.29.6) W 3332—1107 100,000 10/13 H W V Forms/C. 2118/10.

Army Form C. 2118.

WAR DIARY
or
~~INTELLIGENCE SUMMARY.~~
(Erase heading not required.)

Instructions regarding War Diaries and Intelligence Summaries are contained in F.S. Regs., Part II. and the Staff Manual respectively. Title pages will be prepared in manuscript.

Hour, Date, Place	Summary of Events and Information	Remarks and references to Appendices
VERMELLES 14.10.15	Bttn. Ration stables during afternoon & forward guns (2 117 Battery) brought back after dark from forward position at G.17.d.12 & Lost position at G.12.c.9.4	REF. MAP TRENCH MAP 36. S.N.W. 3 & pt.of 1 BETHUNE 1/40,000
15.10.15	One Section from rear battery taken out after dark and replaced by 2 [illegible] section of Batteries from the 6th Division (T.F.) viz: 72nd Brigade.	
16.10.15	Running Examination of back Batteries taken and after dark -- Both Batteries marched to Biette on a Poisoning after dark, on a convey ou N/October and going into rest.	
LAPUGNOY 17.10.15	Ad rest in Biette	
16.10.15	Both Batteries marched to MARLE-LES-MINES to Biette	Capt Lord W.m Graham posted to 116 Bty. 17/10/15.

Army Form C. 2118.

WAR DIARY
or
INTELLIGENCE SUMMARY
(Erase heading not required.)

Hour, Date, Place	Summary of Events and Information	Remarks and references to Appendices
LAPUGNOY MARLE-LES-MINES 19.10.15	Both Batteries marched to LIÈRES to Billets	Lt. H Thomas posted to 1st D.A.C. 25/10/15 off 24/10/15
LIÈRES 20.10.15	Both Batteries in Billets at rest at LIÈRES	R.S.M. Stanley promoted & unit stuck from 11/10/15 proceeded to Base 27/10/15
to 31.10.15	Remained at LIÈRES to rest	Cadr a.v.S. Napier posted to 117th Bty 29/10/15

C.B. Hamm Lt. Col R.F.A
Comdg 26" Bde R.F.A

1st Division

26 Bde R.F.A.
Nov / Vol XVI

121/767

On app.

26th Brigade R.F.A.

Army Form C. 2118.

WAR DIARY
or
INTELLIGENCE SUMMARY.
(Erase heading not required.)

Instructions regarding War Diaries and Intelligence Summaries are contained in F.S. Regs., Part II. and the Staff Manual respectively. Title pages will be prepared in manuscript.

Hour, Date, Place	Summary of Events and Information	Remarks and references to Appendices
LIÈRES Nov 1st to Nov 13/15	Both Batteries billeted in billets at LIÈRES.	Ref. TRENCH MAP 36.c.N.W.3
13.11.15	Marched to billets at MARLES LES MINES.	
FOSSE 7 15.11.15	On arrival 116 Battery took up position after dark at G.27.a.5.5. as closely through close to FOSSE 7. On arrival 117 Battery took into position after dark at G.33.0.2.9. (S. of FOSSE 7) Both Batteries ingoing in the HINTON GROUP. Both Batteries registering on [illegible] One other registered & road Battery brought up afterwards.	9H. O.P. Livingstone R.F.A. posted to 117 Bty 9/11/- [illegible] 2H. C.V. Cunning R.F.A. posted to 117 D.S.C. as Adjutant 6.11.15
16.11.15		
17.11.15	Completed. Two wireoned pits being dug by road 1 Bty. Bombarded [illegible] trenches by both Bty. c 11.0 a.m. and 11.20 a.m. (3) counter fire Bty and Boche, no action on enemy trenches.	

Forms/C. 2118/10.

Army Form C. 2118.

WAR DIARY
or
INTELLIGENCE SUMMARY.
(Erase heading not required.)

Instructions regarding War Diaries and Intelligence Summaries are contained in F.S. Regs., Part II. and the Staff Manual respectively. Title pages will be prepared in manuscript.

Hour, Date, Place	Summary of Events and Information	Remarks and references to Appendices
FOSSE 7 18.11.15	Bombardment by 117 Bty. at 12.15 on enemy trenches at H.25.c.6.5.- H.25.c.7.5. Rounds fired 36 per Bty. No 3 minor enemy interested on our front line trenches. Bombardment by 16 Bty. at 3.20.p.m. on H.13.d.3.9.-3.7 Enemy retaliated on our front trenches at 116.B.7. Enemy [illegible] Bombardments [illegible] on [illegible] replied. Opened fire. Bombardments [illegible]	Ref. TRENCH MAP 36.c.N.W.3 1/10,000
19.11.15	Enemy [illegible] front line and communication trenches, and front line war 116.B.7. [illegible] 5.9". How. shell's fire [illegible] quietly shewed. No damage. Bombarded by our [illegible] H.13.d.7.5-8.5 both Btys. 36 Rounds each. 3 minor [illegible]	
20.11.15 3.5 p.m.	At 11.3.55 a.m. Bombardment of [illegible] H.25.d.6½.9 by both Btys. 36 Rounds per Bty in 2 min. Enemy replied [illegible]	

Forms/C. 2118/10.

Army Form C. 2118.

WAR DIARY
or
INTELLIGENCE SUMMARY.
(Erase heading not required.)

Instructions regarding War Diaries and Intelligence Summaries are contained in F.S. Regs., Part II. and the Staff Manual respectively. Title pages will be prepared in manuscript.

Hour, Date, Place	Summary of Events and Information	Remarks and references to Appendices
FOSSE 7 20.11.15 cont.	116 Bty. kept up night fire at 3 minute intervals on Com. Trenches at L.4.R.C. and H.19.b (90 Rounds)	Ref. TRENCH MAP 36.C.N.W.S
21.11.15	Rest Bty. retaliating for enemy shelling any Bombing for 3 minutes by Rt & Lt Bty. (3 minutes each). Bty fired 4.13 a.m - 7.55. Enemy special not retaliated. 117 Bty. fired rounds at Trench at G.5 corner from I.30 m. tie outside rail. Very thick weather. Few rounds fired by each Bty. at hostile trench.	
22.11.15		
23.11.15	116 Bty. attended to SCOTT GROUP fire shots out gives a new zone from G.2.0.2.6 to G.12.a.6.6 116 Bty. registering on Hun's gun emplacement on. 117 Bty. fired a few rounds in retaliation for Hun shelling.	2nd Lt. R.J. Stevens (174 (Rochdale) Bly RFA) attached to 116 Bty for course instruction from 23/11/15

WAR DIARY or INTELLIGENCE SUMMARY.

(Erase heading not required.)

Army Form C. 2118.

Hour, Date, Place	Summary of Events and Information	Remarks and references to Appendices
FOSSE 7 24.11.15	Col. 11th Sqn. 117 Bty. Bombarded for 8 minutes mill. 76 Reinforced away from Cross Road at Puits. 14 bis. A few rounds fired in retaliation.	REF TRENCH MAP 36.C.N.W.3
25.11.15	During the day by both Batteys. Both Battys fired during day on Saps, fires from line over unusual distance track registration.	Observation O.P. 1 (Avenue)
3.15 p.m	Bombarded (75 rounds) by 117 Bty. enemy fired one round at H.25.c.77	
26.11.15	116 Bty. retaliated night fg during day. 116 Bty. shell having in Grenery shed. 85 H.E. shells. In daylight. 117 Bty. retaliated for enemy shelling during day (about 170 rounds)	2.H. 25. Former PFA 15 R.O.E. April (?) 111 Rpt. for October forward 25/11/15
27.11.15	116 Bty. retaliated during day of Bombarded night. 1 HULLUCH at 7 am with 50 H.E. 117 Bty. fired with 5.9 for demolition /WINGLES (to count Rd) 117 Bty. bombarded trenches H.30.d.11.6.4.-11.2.7/z	Correlation O.R.1 (Avenue)

Army Form C. 2118.

WAR DIARY
or
INTELLIGENCE SUMMARY.
(Erase heading not required.)

Hour, Date, Place	Summary of Events and Information	Remarks and references to Appendices
FOSSE 7 28.11.15	116 intermittent moderately during day for enemy shelling. 116 Bty having shelled during day about 5" 9 from direction WINGLES. Bombarded Q5 minutes) entrance H.25.d.9.9 to H.25.c.1.9 by 117 Bty. 117 Bty retaliated occasionally during day from hostile shelling. 116 Bty. retaliation for enemy hostile shelling.	Ref. TRENCH MAP 36. c.N.W. 3 ½
3.30 pm		
29.11.15	during the day 116 Bty bombarded HULLOCH on 100 rounds from 6.30 p.m. to 5.0 a.m. At 7 a.m. 117 Bty bombarded junction H.26.c.0.6 - 2½.6½ Communication trench all day about 20 rounds	
30.11.15	116 fairly quiet all day 117 Bty bombarded at H.3.R. with 75" rounds to enemy trenches H.25.c.7.4-7.5½ Observer fire for such.	

C.D.Murphy
Lt. Col.
CMdg 26.B.A.

26th Bde. R.F.A.

See Vol XVII

1st Div

WAR DIARY or INTELLIGENCE SUMMARY

Army Form C. 2118.

26th Brigade R.F.A.

Hour, Date, Place	Summary of Events and Information	Remarks and references to Appendices
FOSSE 7 1.12.15	Inaccurate retaliation by 116th Bty. during day. At 3.15 p.m. 116th Bty. bombarded (75 rounds) trenches in H.7.a.1.6. 116th Bty. trigger lines shelled at NOEUX-LES-MINES. 117th Bty. retaliated rather heavily for enemy shelling during day (170 rounds).	Reference TRENCH MAP 36.c.N.W.3 1/10,000. At 9.41 a.m. 7 O.R. wounded (one slightly remaining on duty). 5. S.D. Smart killed.
2.12.15	At 2 p.m. 116th Bty. bombarded enemy trenches at H.13.d.5.5 - 4.4. At 10 a.m. 117th Bty. bombarded with 75 rounds enemy trenches H.25.c.9½.7 - d.1.7. Comparatively little shelling by enemy during day. Fairly heavy retaliation by both batteries during day.	
3.12.15	Very little firing by 116th Bty. Neighbourhood of 116th Bty. (QUALITY STREET) heavily shelled with 5.9 How. shells during day. No damage done.	
4.12.15	At 11 a.m. 117th Bty. bombarded wood in H.26.a. and c. Fairly heavy retaliation by 117 Bty. during day.	

Army Form C. 2118.

WAR DIARY
or
INTELLIGENCE SUMMARY.
(Erase heading not required.)

Hour, Date, Place	Summary of Events and Information	Remarks and references to Appendices
FOSSE 7 5.12.15	At 3.0 and at 3.30 p.m. 117th Bty bombarded front line trenches at H.25.b. and H.25.d. (75 rounds) Fairly heavy retaliation during day. Comparatively quiet retaliation by 116th Bty. Vicinity of FOSSE 7 shelled intermittently from 1 p.m. to 7 p.m. during day. 20 damaged houses.	Reference TRENCH MAP 36.C.N.W.3 1/10,000
6.12.15	At 3 p.m. 116th Bty. bombarded trenches at H.7.9.0.a. – 7.0 (75 rounds) 116th Bty. was again shelled heavily during day from an easterly direction, also from CITE ST. ELIE. No damage. At 11.15 a.m. 117th Bty bombarded enemy trenches at H.19.d. (75 rounds). Considerable heavy retaliation during day.	
7.12.15	At 10 a.m. 116th Bty. bombarded front line trenches in their zone. Considerable retaliation by both batteries during day.	2 Lt. E.J. Good R.F.A. (Reserve Brigade) R.F.A. attached for course of instruction to 116th Bty.) left for England

WAR DIARY
INTELLIGENCE SUMMARY
(Erase heading not required.)

Army Form C. 2118.

Instructions regarding War Diaries and Intelligence Summaries are contained in F.S. Regs., Part II. and the Staff Manual respectively. Title pages will be prepared in manuscript.

Hour, Date, Place	Summary of Events and Information	Remarks and references to Appendices
FOSSE 7		Reference: TRENCH MAP 36.C.N.W.3. 1/10000
8.12.15	At 10 a.m. 118th Bty. bombarded trenches in H.13.C. 50 rounds H.E. QUALITY STREET (116th Bty.) was heavily shelled between 12 and 1 p.m. and between 2 and 3.30 p.m. with 5.9 shells from DOUVRIN. No damage and no response whatever.	
9.12.15	118th Bty. retaliated for two Lonsdale bombardments by 117th Bty. during day, emptying each about 7 rounds. At 2.0 p.m. and at 3.15.b.m. 117th Bty. bombarded the enemy front trenches in H.13.C. Desultory retaliation during day.	2/Lt. J.S. Thomas R.F.A. left 117th Bty. for hospital (sick).
10.12.15	At 1 p.m. 116th Bty. retaliated with 50 rounds for enemy bombardment of our front line, support and water supply trenches. At 12.15 and 3 p.m. 117th Bty. bombarded with 175 rounds of H.E. road line the enemy front trenches at H.19.a.6.0 and at H.19.a.9.3. A trench 50 yards long was bombarded and at H.19.c.9.3. About 50 yards long. Fairly heavy retaliation by batteries during day.	

WAR DIARY
or
INTELLIGENCE SUMMARY
(Erase heading not required.)

Army Form C. 2118.

Hour, Date, Place	Summary of Events and Information	Remarks and references to Appendices
FOSSE 7 & VERMELLES 11.12.15	Registered retaliation by 116 Bty. Heavy retaliation by 117 Bty during day (176 rounds) After dark one section of 116 Bty moved its new position at VERMELLES (G.1.b.0.5.)	Reference: TRENCH MAP 36.C.N.W.3 1/10000
12.12.15	Registered retaliation by both Batteries. 116 Bty registered section in new position. From 6.30 p.m. to 7.45 p.m. 117 Bty fired salvoes of shrapnel on trenches at H.20.a.5.1 to H.20.b.5.1	
13.12.15	From this date Col. HINTON C.C.B. took command of SCOTT GROUP (hereafter called LEFT GROUP) consisting of 113 B, 114 B, 115 B and 116 B Batteries, and Col. MACNAGHTON D.S.O. took command of HINTON GROUP (hereafter called RIGHT GROUP) consisting of 64, 51, 54 B and 117 B Batteries. Registered retaliation by 117 Bty during day. From 3.0 p.m. to 6.0 p.m. 117 Bty bombarded at 3 minute intervals zone bounded on H.19.9.8.0 and 6.0 yards N. Zone covered by LEFT GROUP from VENDIN ALLEY (H.19.9.1.8) to DEVON LANE (G.1.26.2.2.)	Capt. G.P.Brown R.F.A. 26 B DAC left on leave to England

WAR DIARY / INTELLIGENCE SUMMARY

Army Form C. 2118.

Reference: TRENCH MAP 36.C.N.W.3. 1/10000

Hour, Date, Place	Summary of Events and Information	Remarks and references to Appendices
FOSSE 7 & VERMELLES		
14.12.15	This group front 1 Left Brigade 8 Division. 116th and 115th Bys. cover Right Bde. and 117th and 118th cover the Left Bde.	
15.12.15	Moderate retaliation by 116th Bty during day. Fairly heavy retaliation by 117th Bty during day. 118th Bty firing quiet, very little retaliation. 117th Bty retaliated extensively (155 rounds) for hostile shelling in support area.	2 Lt. J.S. Spencer R.F.A. rejoined 117th Bty from hospital.
16.12.15	Fairly heavy retaliation by 116th Bty during day, about 230 rounds. From 6 p.m. to midnight 118th Bty bombarded trench in G.12.b.6.1 with 90 rounds in 10 mins. 118th & 116th Bys deliberately bombarded retaliation by 117th Bty during day.	
17.12.15	About 50 rounds retaliation by 116 & 118th Bty during day. From 11 a.m. to 11 p.m. 116th Bty deliberately shelled trench G.12.d.9½.9 – H.7.c.0.7 with 230 rounds H.E. 117th Bty did not fire — light very bad.	

WAR DIARY
or
INTELLIGENCE SUMMARY.
(Erase heading not required.)

Army Form C. 2118.

Instructions regarding War Diaries and Intelligence Summaries are contained in F.S. Regs., Part II. and the Staff Manual respectively. Title pages will be prepared in manuscript.

Hour, Date, Place	Summary of Events and Information	Remarks and references to Appendices
FOSSE 7 & VERMELLES		Reference: TRENCH MAP 36.C.N.W.3. 1/10,000
18.12.15	116 Bty. retaliated on enemy intermittently during day. 117 Bty. did not fire. Light enemy front line strength.	
19.12.15	116 Bty. very quiet. Very little shooting. 117 Bty. at 11.0 a.m. bombarded with 125 rounds enemy front line trenches. Fairly heavy retaliation during day.	
20.12.15	Light but persistently to firing.	20.12.15. L. Hall (Commander Regt.) (attached to 116 Bty for course of instruction) joined.
21.12.15	Fairly heavy retaliation during day by 116 Bty. from 9 p.m. to 3 a.m. 116 Bty. bombarded usual junction G.12.b.5.1. (90 rounds)	
22.12.15	116 Bty. bombarded usual at H.13 with 75 rounds at 11.10 a.m. 117 Bty. retaliated very little. Fairly quiet. 116 Bty. retaliated very little during day (7 rounds)	2.O.R. (117 Bty) wounded but remained on duty.
23.12.15	0/12.15 p.m. 117 Bty bombarded usual H.20.C.3.2.9.4. H.20.9.1.1. with 62 shrapnel and 6 5 H.E. Heavy retaliation also during day (about 400 rounds). Fairly heavy retaliation 117 & 116 Bty during day for hostile shelling of communication & support trenches	
24.12.15		

WAR DIARY
INTELLIGENCE SUMMARY
(Erase heading not required.)

Army Form C. 2118.

Hour, Date, Place	Summary of Events and Information	Remarks and references to Appendices
FOSSE 7 & VERMELLES	24.12.15 (contd.) At 12 noon 117th Bty. bombarded Puits 14 bis with 37 rounds H.E. The Boches afterwards manning of their shoot. Desultory retaliation.	Reference: TRENCH MAP 36.C.N.W.3. 1/10,000
	25.12.15 Very quiet day. No rounds fired.	
	26.12.15 118th Bty. Quiet. Very few rounds retaliation. 117th Bty. also fairly quiet.	Lt. Hoeppefforten Regt.)(attested for course of instruction) Sept.
	27.12.15 Considerable retaliation by 116th Bty. for hostile shelling. 117th Bty. retaliated rather heavily (170 rounds) during day. At 7.10 p.m. 2 salvoes were fired at enemy front line trenches in H.19.a.9.4.	Lt. R.H.Littcock R.F.A. (117th Bty.) went to Hospital (sick). 2.O.R. (117th Bty.) wounded (one evening at duty)
	28.12.15 Rounds retaliation by 116th Bty. during day. 117th Bty. retaliated vigorously during day for hostile shelling of our front and supports. Considerable retaliation during the day by 116th Bty.	
	29.12.15 117th Bty. shelled enemy front line trenches fairly heavily during day in retaliation for hostile shelling.	

WAR DIARY
INTELLIGENCE SUMMARY
(Erase heading not required.)

Army Form C. 2118.

Hour, Date, Place	Summary of Events and Information	Remarks and references to Appendices
FOSSE 7 & VERMELLES 30.12.15.	Reports received during day by 116 & Bty. up to 4.15 p.m. At 4.30 p.m. report was received from Bty. H.Q. that 2 mines had been sprung in G.12.9.8.5 and that support and reserve lines were being shelled. A steady rate of fire was kept up by 116 Bty. until 5.40 p.m. when report was received all quiet. Rounds fired 360 Shrapnel 56 H.E.	Reference: TRENCH MAP 36.C.N.W.3. 1/10,000 Capt. Trotter R.F.A. (attached to Group for course of Instruction) joined.
31.12.15.	Very unfavourable observation by 117 & Bty. during day on their front especially where enemy opened fire after minor explosion. Very little firing by 116 & Bty. during day 2 rounds registration by 117 & Bty. At 10.30 a.m. 117 Bty fired 2 rounds on trench in H.19.a.6.6 At 7 a.m. 75 rounds were fired on trench at PUITS 12 B15 At 11.6 p.m. 5 rounds were fired on trench at H.19.9.6.3	

C. D. M????
Lt. Col. R.F.A.
Cd. 3. 265 Div. R.F.A.

1ST DIVISION

H.Q.,
26TH BRIGADE R.F.A.
JAN - DEC 1916

1st Divisional Artillery.

H. Q. 26th BRIGADE R.F.A. :: JANUARY 1916.

WAR DIARY
or
INTELLIGENCE SUMMARY

Army Form C. 2118

26th Brigade R.F.A.

Place	Date	Hour	Summary of Events and Information	Remarks and references to Appendices
VERMELLES & FOSSE 7	1/1/16		116th Bty fired very little (only 19 rounds) Fairly heavy retaliation during day by 117th Bty (128 rounds) for hostile shelling of communication trenches	Reference TRENCH MAP 36/c NW3 1/10,000
	2/1		116th Bty fired salvos of 12 rounds at 10 am 11.30 am and 7 pm also light retaliation during day for hostile shelling. Moderate retaliation by 117th Bty during day	
	3/1		Considerable retaliation by 116th Bty during day (97 rounds). 117th Bty retaliated with 46 rounds for hostile shelling of our communication trenches. 117th Bty shelled during afternoon with 5.9 shells & cream crackers	Casualties 2 O.R. wounded (remained at duty)
	4/1		Considerable retaliation by 116th Bty during day (64 rounds) Bad light most of day observation difficult. 117th Bty bombarded trenches round PUITS 14 BIS at 9.15 pm and at 12.10 am with 127 Shrapnel and 98 H.E. Moderate retaliation by 117th Bty (51 rounds) during day. Considerable shelling in retaliation by 116th Bty during day (81 rounds)	
	5/1		9.15 pm, 9.45 pm, 10.30 pm and 12-5 am, 117th Bty bombarded trenches round PUITS 14 bis with 80 rounds each time. Very little retaliation by 117th Bty during day Moderate retaliation by 116th Bty during day (45 rounds)	Casualties 2 O.R. killed 3 O.R. wounded (remained at duty)
	6/1		Very little retaliation by 117th Bty during day (20 rounds)	

Army Form C. 2118

WAR DIARY
or
INTELLIGENCE SUMMARY
(Erase heading not required.)

Instructions regarding War Diaries and Intelligence Summaries are contained in F. S. Regs., Part II. and the Staff Manual respectively. Title Pages will be prepared in manuscript.

Place	Date	Hour	Summary of Events and Information	Remarks and references to Appendices
VERMELLES & FOSSE 7	7/1		116th Bty retaliated freely heavily during day for hostile shelling of our support and communication trenches (71 rounds) Moderate retaliation during day by 117th Bty. At 4 pm 117th Bty was shelled by 4.2" shells from CITÉ ST ELIE	
	8/1		116th Bty zone received considerable attention from hostile batteries during day. We fired in retaliation (166 rounds) Considerable retaliation by 117th Bty during day (93 rounds)	
	9/1		Fairly heavy shelling of our support and communication trenches by enemy during day. 116th Bty retaliated with 85 rounds. Considerable shelling of communication trenches in 117th Bty zone during day, to which 117th Bty replied. During night of 9th–10th a regular and sustained bombardment to programme was carried out by us covering a bombing enterprise by party of 2nd K.R.R. against PUITS 14 BIS. This shooting was observed from front trenches and proved to be very accurate and effective.	
	10/1		CHAPEL ALLEY, DEVON LANE & front line trenches shelled fairly heavily by enemy during the day. 116th retaliated effectively with (129 rounds) Very considerable shelling in 117th Bty zone during day, particularly on the support and communication trenches, we retaliated on enemy front line and communication trench H 19.8 (81 rounds)	

WAR DIARY or INTELLIGENCE SUMMARY

Army Form C. 2118

Place	Date	Hour	Summary of Events and Information	Remarks and references to Appendices
VERMELLES & FOSSE 7	11/1		Not much shelling by enemy on 116th Bty zone. 116th Bty fired at hostile working parties and at hostile H.I. 9.0.7½ suspected headquarters. Rather heavy shelling during day by enemy on front and communication trenches in 117th Bty zone. 117th retaliated (87 rounds)	
	12/1		Much shelling of support and communication trenches in 116th Bty zone during day. Also enemy were very active with rifle grenades and trench mortars. About 80 % of H.V. 2" fired on DEVON LANE were blind. Also 20% of 9 trench mortar rounds were blind. 116th Bty retaliated with 110 rounds. Fairly quiet day on 117th Bty zone.	
	13/1		Three bursts of 12 rounds H.E. each fired by 116th Bty at 11-30 a.m, 3 p.m and 7 p.m. otherwise very quiet day. A quiet day on 117th Bty zone.	
	14/1		A good deal of trench mortaring and rifle grenading of our front line also in 116th Bty zone during day. 116th Bty retaliated with 144 rounds including 20 rounds fired at hostile working party. Slight bombardment of our front trenches and communication trenches in 117th Bty zone. 117th Bty replied with 26 rounds.	
	15/1		Quiet day. Section of each battery relieved by section of 72nd Bde and 71st Bde at 5-30 p.m.	

Army Form C. 2118

WAR DIARY
or
INTELLIGENCE SUMMARY
(Erase heading not required.)

Instructions regarding War Diaries and Intelligence Summaries are contained in F.S. Regs., Part II. and the Staff Manual respectively. Title Pages will be prepared in manuscript.

Place	Date	Hour	Summary of Events and Information	Remarks and references to Appendices
VERMELLES & FOSSE 7	16/1		Quiet misty day. Remainder of Batteries relieved by 5-30 pm and whole Brigade moved to billets in AUCHEL moving in different parties. The B.A.C. at 2 pm. wagon lines at 3 pm and batteries on retiring.	Lt. V.R. Allen. Bec Ad posted to 39th Dev. Bde 28/1/16. Lt. R.H. Ludorke 117th B.5 posted to 25th B. de 13 Dev. Bde. 25-1-16. Lt. D.F. McConnell 113th B.5 joined & posted to 117th.
	17/1 to 31/1		Resting at AUCHEL in I 4 b. After a general clean up battery training was carried on.	

C. Minton Maj RFA
Commdg 26th Dev RFA

1st Divisional Artillery.

26th BRIGADE R.F.A. ::: FEBRUARY 1916.

February 1916   Army Form C. 2118

WAR DIARY
or
INTELLIGENCE SUMMARY
(Erase heading not required.)

26th Brigade R.F.A.

Place	Date	Hour	Summary of Events and Information	Remarks and references to Appendices
AUCHEL	From 1st to 15th		Brigade in reserve at AUCHEL.	MAP 36 B 1/40,000 and TRENCH MAP 36.C.S.W.1 1/10,000
	16		The section east of 116 and 117 Batteries moved into positions after dark at LES BREBIS, relieving batteries of 47th (London) Division. 116th Battery relieved 13th London Battery out at G.31.d.2½.1. 117th Bty relieved 9th London Bty at L.36.c.2.9.	R.1.16 3 H. 40 PILE relieved 116 Bty & Section 1.2.04 G.1.16 2H.
LES BREBIS	17		Day spent in negotiating new group. After dark remaining sections of 116 and 117 Btys. came into action. Lt. Col. F.S. Hinton C.M.G. commanded LEFT GROUP consisting of 113, 114, 115, and 116 Batteries covering LOOS SECTOR (LEFT SIDE) of 1st Division. Joined LOOS SECTOR from M.5.9.3.2 to LOOS-ST. LAURENT ROAD. 117 Bty was in RIGHT GROUP commanded by Lt. Col. E.A Hanaghton & CO. LEFT GROUP H.Q. at LES BREBIS G.29.c.7.5. Battery waggon lines at FOSSE 2 DE BETHUNE (L.15.C)	R.H. SALTMARSH attended for instruction with units relieving
	18		Fairly quiet day. Both Batteries shoot the day in registering new zones.	F.1.16 Capt J.D.G. MACNEECE reported to [illegible] 1877.

Army Form C. 2118

WAR DIARY
or
INTELLIGENCE SUMMARY
(Erase heading not required.)

Instructions regarding War Diaries and Intelligence Summaries are contained in F.S. Regs., Part II. and the Staff Manual respectively. Title Pages will be prepared in manuscript.

Place	Date	Hour	Summary of Events and Information	Remarks and references to Appendices
LES BREBIS	19		Considerable retaliation during day by 116 & 117 for hostile shelling (120 rounds)	TRENCH MAP 36.C.S.W.1 1/10000
	20		Quiet day on 117th Bty Zone. Hostile T.M. engaged during afternoon and silenced. 116th Bty fired 90 rounds in retaliation during the day. From 1.30 to 3.30 p.m. 116th Bty was heavily shelled with 5.9 shell from ST. AUGUSTE. 20 casualties and no damage done.	
	21	1.15 p.m.	Very quiet day on 117th Bty Zone. Sharp shelling of our front line trenches in 116th Bty Zone N. of LENS ROAD and along spare trenches	
		1 pm to 5 pm	116th Bty position and WIGAN generally shelled heavily with 5.9 and gas shells. Repeated 5.30 p.m. to 7.15 p.m.	
	22		Very quiet day on 117th Bty Zone. Very little retaliation. Light enemy trench mortar during the day. A certain amount of hostile fire from shelling 18 pr. trench mortars in 116th Bty Zone. Also a minnenwerfer was active against our front trenches firing from about 17.S.C. 3½. 3R. 116th Bty retaliated. Very quiet day on 117th Bty Zone	

Army Form C. 2118

WAR DIARY
or
INTELLIGENCE SUMMARY
(Erase heading not required.)

Instructions regarding War Diaries and Intelligence Summaries are contained in F.S. Regs., Part II. and the Staff Manual respectively. Title Pages will be prepared in manuscript.

Place	Date	Hour	Summary of Events and Information	Remarks and references to Appendices
LES BREBIS	Feb. 23		Light enemy indifferent during the day. Our front trenches in 116th Bty zone shelled considerably during the day by H.V.G. and trench mortars. 116th Bty. retaliated during the day.	TRENCH MAP 36 to SW1
	24		Shelled during the day with 5.9 from CITE ST AUGUSTE. No change in our zone. Nothing to report from 117th Bty.	23.2.16 1 O.R. wounded (eighty) on duty
	25		Very quiet day. Nothing to report from either battery. Light day during the day. Very little activity.	
		7pm.	At this time we observed a mine by HARTS CRATER (M.6.c.8.9). This was signal for all batteries of 1st Div. to open fire on arranged targets. (Copy of LEFT GROUP orders attached). For instance 91st Flounders attacked HARTS Crater, left boundary lined up by M.G. fire from SUNKEN ROAD (M.6.c.9.8). Right boundary was covered in stop-blocking themselves on S. side of crater. During night enemy blocked no but had sentries & rushes quantity of wire. By beginning a fine sunlit warm day completed all round crater. A slow rate 1 shell was kept up by batteries of left group after position was taken until 9.30 p.m.	
	26		Fairly Quiet day as far as Cratrice shelling was concerned. Enemy	

WAR DIARY or INTELLIGENCE SUMMARY

Army Form C. 2118

(Erase heading not required.)

Instructions regarding War Diaries and Intelligence Summaries are contained in F. S. Regs., Part II. and the Staff Manual respectively. Title Pages will be prepared in manuscript.

Place	Date	Hour	Summary of Events and Information	Remarks and references to Appendices
LES BREBIS	26/2 con.		12 noon onwards 4.2 Cooper Heavy Howr. (9.2") bombarded German front line trench from LOOS CRASSIER to the LENS ROAD joining about 100 rounds. Their shooting appeared very effective and considerable damage to enemy parapet and wire also. Two batteries of Light Trench Mortars a Helluin Wood bombarded on three known areas from 11.0 – 11.30 a.m. (40 rounds per battery). During heavy bombardment fire of Light Trench Mortar communication trenches in rear cut and withdrawal in rear cut off but observed. Quiet day on 117th Bdy. Zone	TRENCH MAP 36.c.S.W.I. 1/10,000
	27		Certain amount of shelling in retaliation by both batteries during the day. In the early morning there was considerable unusual working of our howitzers from behind HARTS and HARRISONS Craters. Our batteries retaliated on suspected locations.	22.2.16 Capt R.P.H. Jackson ordered to H.Q. night 11/12/17 from 113 Bdy.
	28		Light woolly mist forbid observation. During early day otherwise silent in our zone. 11.0 A.M. battery bombarded and blowing up shown ruined buildings during day with 4.2" guns from CITÉ ST AUGUSTE	16.2.16 Capt Scott R.H. Frauenst. back to 3 Bde H.
	29		Quiet day on both batteries zones	14.7.40 Capture amounts for H.Q. 14.7.30 A.Es. ordered (?) back from 1 – 3 B.G.C.

C. Smyth G.S. Col
Col 126 th Bdu.

Operation Orders Left Group

3rd Inf. Bde. attack on HARTS CRATER on 25/11/16

1. At 7pm a mine will be blown up. This will be the signal for 1st Gloucesters to attack and also the signal for 1st Divl Arty to form a barrage and open fire.

2. The Left Group batteries will barrage the front line as under :-

   116 Battery
   From Lens Rd – M6c 9.7 with a gun on Snipers House firing shrapnel

   113 Battery
   From M6c 9.8 (where road Loos-Puits 12 crosses German front line) to M6b 4½.½. firing shrapnel

   114 Battery
   1 gun on front line trench M6b 4.2 to M6b 4½.½. firing shrapnel
   Remainder on front line trench M6c 9.8 to M6b 4½.½. firing HE

   115 Battery
   Lens Rd (1 gun on Snipers House) to M6c 9.7 all firing HE
   (Lone gun not to fire)

3. Rate of fire will be Battery fire 10 secs

Cont:-

"A" Form. Army Form C. 2121.
MESSAGES AND SIGNALS.
No. of Message _____

Prefix _____ Code _____ m.	Words	Charge		This message is on a/c of:	Recd. at _____ m.
Office of Origin and Service Instructions.	Sent				Date _____
_____	At _____ m.		_____ Service.	From _____
_____	To _____			
_____	By _____		(Signature of "Franking Officer.")	By _____

TO {
_____
_____
_____
}

| * | Sender's Number | Day of Month | In reply to Number | **A A A** |

From				
Place				
Time				

The above may be forwarded as now corrected. (Z)

Censor. Signature of Addressor or person authorised to telegraph in his name.

* This line should be erased if not required.

4. Forward Officer 113 Bty will arrange for a telephone line from L.Bn. H.Q. to fighting station of O.C. 1st Gloucesters, and report completion of this. He will be with O.C. 1st Gloucesters and report progress constantly direct to O.C. Left Group.

5. B.C's will check registration so as to ensure accurate shooting at 7 p.m. If necessary, fresh registration must be selected from LOOS CRASSIER.

6. O.C. Left Group will be at Group H.Q.

7. Acknowledge receipt.

Sgd Adj Left Group.

1st Divisional Artillery.

H. Q. 26th BRIGADE R.F.A. ::: MARCH 1916.

Army Form C. 2118

WAR DIARY
or
INTELLIGENCE SUMMARY

(Erase heading not required.)

March 1916   26th Brigade R.F.A.

Instructions regarding War Diaries and Intelligence Summaries are contained in F.S. Regs., Part II. and the Staff Manual respectively. Title Pages will be prepared in manuscript.

Place	Date	Hour	Summary of Events and Information	Remarks and references to Appendices
LES BREBIS	1		Comparatively quiet day on both Battery zones. A little retaliation by hostile T.M. active during morning between HARTS and HAWKINS Craters. Batteries no retaliation.	Ref. TRENCH MAP 36.C.S.W.1 None
	2		Quiet day on 116th Battery zone. Observation poor but no movement visible. Enemy fired a number of single rounds on front trenches in 117th Bty zone, apparently registering. Battery retaliated.	1/3/16 to 17/3/16 CAPT STOCKFORD S. MIDLAND Bde attached 117 Bty
	3		Observation very bad on account of mist. A little sniping on our front and support trenches on 117th Bty zone to which Battery fired in retaliation.	
	4		Quiet day. A little shelling on 117th Bty zone. A little shelling on 73 and 1 DOUBLE CRASSIER with 5.9. Enemy T.M. active during morning on trenches in No.C. Considerable hostile artillery activity on 116th Bty zone.	
	5		About 70 rounds were fired in retaliation during the morning. N end 1 DOUBLE CRASSIER was shelled with 4.2 at intervals. Tramway in Loophere hely of N.9.6. trip trenched during afternoon. About 100 rounds fired by 117th Bty in retaliation.	

WAR DIARY
or
INTELLIGENCE SUMMARY

(Erase heading not required.)

Army Form C. 2118

Place	Date	Hour	Summary of Events and Information	Remarks and references to Appendices
LES BREBIS	6		Considerable hostile artillery activity on 118 Bty. zone during morning. Langham arc 1 DOUBLE CRASSIER shelled with 4.2 during the morning.	
	7		Enemy day. Trench mortars very difficult. Heavy artillery active on our trenches and battery positions during the day. 116 & Bty trenches shelled with 4.2 apparently from CITÉ ST LAURENT. One gun temporarily put out of action, otherwise no damage done.	I.O.R. wounded (still at duty) 7.4.16.
	9		Very quiet day on 117 Bty. zone. Quiet day on 116. zone. Southern arc of DOUBLE CRASSIER shelled intermittently during morning with 4.2	
	10		Fairly quiet day on both Battery zones except for occasional rounds on front trenches.	
	11		Quiet day. Trench mortars very difficult. Very little activity.	2Lt. J.S. SPENCER to hospital
	12		Hostile artillery active throughout day on DOUBLE CRASSIER and communication trenches on whole division front. Our batteries retaliated.	

Army Form C. 2118

WAR DIARY
or
INTELLIGENCE SUMMARY
(Erase heading not required.)

Instructions regarding War Diaries and Intelligence Summaries are contained in F.S. Regs., Part II. and the Staff Manual respectively. Title Pages will be prepared in manuscript.

Place	Date	Hour	Summary of Events and Information	Remarks and references to Appendices
LES BREBIS	13		Considerable shelling during day on both battery zones. Batteries retaliated.	
	14		The DOUBLE CRASSIER received considerable attention from enemy artillery during the day. The Southern neighbourhood trenches were shelled with 4.2" and 5.9" at different periods of the day.	
	15		Fairly quiet day on both battery zones except a few 4.2" and 77 mm. found themselves close to DOUBLE CRASSIER	2nd/Lt J.S. Spencer rejoined 117 Bty.
	16		Quiet day on both zones	Capt. I.H. Ritchie R.A.M.C. to hospital.
	17		Enemy away observation difficult.	Lt. Proudfoot R.A.M.C. joins 2nd Gd. Bde from 1st F.A.
	18		Cuinchy Avenue shelling. Our front trenches in front battery zones into a great deal of trench bursting on 117	1 S/Sgt B/180 att. 116 Bty 1 Sack D/180 att. 117 Bty
	19		Bty zone and our trenches N.E. DOUBLE CRASSIER 116 Bty fired on and dispersed hostile working parts at 1730.21.4.K. Zones retaliated by both batteries during the day.	
	20		Intense retaliation by both batteries at 7.45.6 a. CRASSIER BARRAGE was opened up by 117 Bty, on enemy seen from front line going up to DOUBLE CRASSIER	

Army Form C. 2118

WAR DIARY
or
INTELLIGENCE SUMMARY
(Erase heading not required.)

Instructions regarding War Diaries and Intelligence Summaries are contained in F. S. Regs., Part II. and the Staff Manual respectively. Title Pages will be prepared in manuscript.

Place	Date	Hour	Summary of Events and Information	Remarks and references to Appendices
LES BREBIS	21		Observation bad throughout the day. Hostile Artillery quiet.	
	22		A quiet day. Observation bad owing to mist.	
	23		Hostile artillery fairly quiet. Trench movement active on our trenches near the DOUBLE CRASSIER. No retaliation.	
	24		At 12.30 p.m. we blew up a tunnel head on S. side of N. arm of DOUBLE CRASSIER. Exchanges for several shelling of our front and support lines. Enemy sniping of rifts prevented in our front.	
	25		116 Bty fired on hostile working party at M.16.J.9 and dispersed them. Otherwise a quiet day.	
	26		Visibility rather good throughout day. But day was very quiet.	
	27th		Exceptionally quiet day. Observation was very good during the morning. Trench mortars active all day round DOUBLE CRASSIER.	
	28th		Field guns active early in the morning on 116 Bty front. Exchange of light bombs on DOUBLE CRASSIER about midday. Observation fair.	
	29th		More hostile artillery activity than usual especially about HARRISON'S crater with 5.9" though shooting was very bad. 117 Bty retaliated from its alternative positions G.31.d.04. and M.1.b.2.8.	

Army Form C. 2118

WAR DIARY
or
INTELLIGENCE SUMMARY
(Erase heading not required.)

Place	Date	Hour	Summary of Events and Information	Remarks and references to Appendices
Les Brebis	30th		Quiet day.	
	31st	6.35am	Enemy exploded small a mine on Harrison's Crater and between 8.30 and 8.40 shelled M5b heavily with 77mm. More hostile artillery activity than usual. Hart's Crater was heavily shelled during the morning. Double Crassier and trenches to S. of it shelled with heavy shells intermittently during the day. Also forward positions shelled heavily at intervals. 116 Bty registered from alternative position M16.8.8.	

C.B.Minter
Lt. Col.
Comdg 26th Bde R.F.A.

1st Divisional Artillery.

H.Q. 26th BRIGADE R.F.A. ::: APRIL 1916.

APRIL 1916

Army Form C. 2118

WAR DIARY
or
INTELLIGENCE SUMMARY

(Erase heading not required.)

26th Brigade R.F.A.

Place	Date	Hour	Summary of Events and Information	Remarks and references to Appendices
LES BREBIS	April 1		Fairly quiet day on 116 A Battery Zone. Considerable shelling with 77 x/n & howitzers in 117 K Bty. Zone. Battery established.	Trench Map. 36c S.W 9°°°
	2		Very heavy shelling of our front line from M.6.c.c.c. to 6.8 with 77 m.m. from 7.15 a.m. to 7.30 a.m. About 150 rounds were fired. From 12 noon onwards the same trenches were shelled with 5.9 shell at rate of 1 per minute. HARTS and HARRISONS craters were also shelled heavily with H.E. during the afternoon. B 117 Bty. fired the 5. a.m. DOUBLE CRAWLER was heavily and rather half-heartedly retaliated and heavy artillery retaliated for heavy shelling of trenches.	
	3		Indiscriminate activity on both battery zones with C.H.V. Hostile trench mortars again fired on S. a.m. DOUBLE CRAWLER after about one minute. (Gas guns which remained in position) of 116th Battery was relieved by no section of C/150. B/16th R.A. Similarly on section of 117 Bty. was relieved by no section of A/150. Both relieved operations (Batteries) were relieved to AMES.	

WAR DIARY or INTELLIGENCE SUMMARY

Army Form C. 2118

Place	Date	Hour	Summary of Events and Information	Remarks and references to Appendices
LES BREBIS	4		Observation rather difficult all day. Very little hostile activity. After dark a further section of road of 116th and 117th Batteries were relaid by section of C/150 and A/150 respectively. Sections of 116 and 117 Batteries (less sub which remained in positions) marched to AMES. One section of road 116 and 117 Batteries were covered in.	
	5		16th D.A. Battery commenced a general withdrawal of batteries during their period of attachment to left group. A little hostile activity with L.H.V. or shrapnel during morning with L.H.V. DOUBLE CRASSIER was shelled during morning. Bty gone.	
	6		HARTS & HARRISONS covered shelled during afternoon with a few H.E. Brick Bays or Mine. and during afternoon with a few H.E. Brick Bays or Mine. 117 Bty. gone.	
	7		Enemy aeroplanes very active; both batteries & trenches heavily shelled in both zones.	
	8		Fewer rounds of hostile with L.H.V. or Shrapnel. Quiet day on whole front.	

WAR DIARY or INTELLIGENCE SUMMARY

Army Form C. 2118

Place	Date	Hour	Summary of Events and Information	Remarks and references to Appendices
LES BREBIS	9		A certain amount of shelling of communication trenches in front of MAROC and MAROC itself with 77.m.m. 117th Battery cut wire in M.10.C.0.4 with 3/1 rounds on preliminary to feint attack by 23rd Div. on our right. Later in the day 2 R.H. fired on KENS Road also on M4 D & M5A. And the front trenches in M5.D.	
	10		Enemy fairly active on front line communication trenches also on MAROC, the 116th Battery retaliated on enemy front line trench. In the 117th Battery zone enemy's fire was normal, except that a heavy minenwerfer was very active on the S. arm of DOUBLE CRASSIER, however not much damage was done, the enemy dropped several shells into his own front line. The 114th Battery took part in a bombardment of the enemy's trenches in front of 23rd Div. on our right, this was part of the scheme for a feint attack by the 23rd Division	
	11		high shelling of our front support trenches with 77 m/m. LOOS was shelled throughout the day, at intervals. We exploded a mine on the N. arm of DOUBLE CRASSIER at 2 p.m. Enemy retaliated with 77 m/m	2nd Lieut W.E. Mitchell left H.Q. for Anti-Aircraft section.

Army Form C. 2118

WAR DIARY
or
INTELLIGENCE SUMMARY
(Erase heading not required.)

Instructions regarding War Diaries and Intelligence Summaries are contained in F.S. Regs., Part II. and the Staff Manual respectively. Title Pages will be prepared in manuscript.

Place	Date	Hour	Summary of Events and Information	Remarks and references to Appendices
LES BREBIS	April 11 (contd)		77m/m. Slight movement was observed opposite an.	Jos hunt R.H. Sastmark att. H.Q. Co.
	12.		light shelling of our trenches. At 116th Battery Zone, this battery retaliated, quiet day on the 114th Battery Zone.	
	13.		Quiet day on both Battery Zones.	
	14.		Enemy active with 77m/m and 4.2's on our support lines and on O.P.'s in MAROC. From 1p.m. to 7p.m. enemy shelled the TOWER BRIDGE in LOOS the NORTHERN tower was knocked down. Our Batteries retaliated on the enemy trenches.	
	15.		Enemy fairly active in early morning with 77m/m on front & support line trenches, our Batteries retaliated.	
	16.		In the 116th Battery Zone, the enemy were active throughout the day with 77m/m, the Battery retaliated. On the 114th Battery Zone, the enemy were active from 8.30 a.m. to 1 p.m. with 77m/m, & heavy minenwerfer, the Battery retaliated, afternoon the remaining TOWER of the LOOS TOWER BRIDGE was knocked down at 3.47 p.m. following this LOOS was shelled with 5.9's.	

WAR DIARY or INTELLIGENCE SUMMARY

Army Form C. 2118

(Erase heading not required.)

Place	Date	Hour	Summary of Events and Information	Remarks and references to Appendices
LES BREBIS.	April 17.		Fairly quiet on the 116th Battery Zone, a small working party was observed and dispersed. On the 117th Battery Zone enemy were active with 77 m & minenwerfer fire damage was done to our trenches in the DOUBLE CRASSIER. At 5 a.m. this Battery retaliated, working party was dispersed. The enemy blew a small mine (camoufle) on the S. arm of DOUBLE CRASSIER. No damage was done to our sap.	
	18.		Enemy were active in the morning on our front support trenches with 77 m/m. The battery retaliated a points on the enemy front line, working parties were seen some distance behind the (the) enemy's trenches. In the 117th Battery Zone, normal. A small camoufle was exploded by us opposite Pie II. between HARRISON'S and HART'S craters.	
	19		Quiet day. We exploded a camoufle at M68 8.8. at 10 a.m.	
	20.		Enemy active in both Battery Zones, in trenches & also a mine buissage in rear, Batteries retaliated for shelling of trenches. LOOS was shelled lightly. Movement was seen more than usual. Ten trenches were shelled 2 117 Bty zone.	
	21.		Enemy active with 77 m/m, 4.2's & 5.9's also trench mortars, on LOOS and our front communication trenches. Enemy also was very active on mine villages behind the line. The Officers Mess & the	

Army Form C. 2118

WAR DIARY
or
INTELLIGENCE SUMMARY
(Erase heading not required.)

Instructions regarding War Diaries and Intelligence Summaries are contained in F.S. Regs., Part II. and the Staff Manual respectively. Title Pages will be prepared in manuscript.

Place	Date	Hour	Summary of Events and Information	Remarks and references to Appendices
LES BREBIS	April 21. (cont.)		76th Bde R.F.A. in LES BREBIS received attention from a 10c.m. H.V. Gun. 13 attacks retaliated. Two observation balloons & aircrafts were seen quite distinctly about 10.000 yds in rear of German line, from 5 by 6". Slight movement observed in hostile trenches.	
	22.		The hostile Artillery was active in the morning on our front support trenches, retaliation was carried out by Batteries. Rain mist all day prevented the enemy from heavily shelling points behind the line.	
	23		The enemy took full advantage of an exceptionally bright day to heavily shell positions behind the line, the 116th Battery position was "strafed" with 4.2"s. 2nd Lieut. W.D. PILE was wounded in the leg and was sent to hospital. Normal amount of shelling of trenches & in which Batteries retaliated. LOOS was also bombarded with various calibre guns & hows, our heavy artillery replied.	2nd Lieut W.D.Pile wounded.
	24		Another very bright day, several German observation balloons up all those undoubtedly directed shelling of various mine villages behind our lines. LOOS was again very heavily shelled. Our batteries retaliated for the normal amount of hostile fire on our trenches, we exploded a mine a SOUTHERN	

WAR DIARY or INTELLIGENCE SUMMARY

Army Form C. 2118

Place	Date	Hour	Summary of Events and Information	Remarks and references to Appendices
LES BREBIS	April 24th (contd)		Arr of DOUBLE CRASSIER at 11.15 p.m. a/tho 73 Brigade.	
	25th		Very quiet day for observation though there was little shelling on our front. The 117 Bty cut wire in M4c and bombarded this at night.	3 Other Ranks wounded (116)
	26th		Misty during early part of morning. Rather heavy trench mortaring of crater in Copse 117 continues wire cutting.	
	27th	5 a.m. to 7 a.m.	Germans bombarded our trenches heavily from HARTS CRATER northwards. No attack developed on our front. Fosse 7 and MAROC and neighbourhood positions were also heavily shelled at intervals during the morning, gas shells being freely used. LES BREBIS also shelled with 10cm. gun while attack on 16th Divs. was in progress.	1 O.R. wounded (117)
	1 p.m. onwards		Remainder of the day was quiet.	
	28th	5 a.m. to 9 a.m.	Considerable artillery fire on LOOS CRASSIER and trenches next wards also FOSSE 7.	
	8.30 a.m.		Enemy barrage trenches by hen's Rd with 77mm and 4.2" at dawn, sending up white lights.	
			Remainder of day fairly quiet.	
	8.40 p.m. to 9.30 p.m.	117 Bty helped in bombarding enemy's trenches in M4c in conjunction with supporting arm. by 2nd Inf Bde.	

Army Form C. 2118

WAR DIARY
or
INTELLIGENCE SUMMARY
(Erase heading not required.)

Instructions regarding War Diaries and Intelligence Summaries are contained in F.S. Regs., Part II. and the Staff Manual respectively. Title Pages will be prepared in manuscript.

Place	Date	Hour	Summary of Events and Information	Remarks and references to Appendices
	29F	4a.m. onwards	Slight shelling of our trenches from Loos CRASSIER northwards. Also FOSSE 7 was shelled from 4 a.m. to 9 a.m. This was in conjunction with enemy's attack on 16th Divn.	2/Lt C.C. Vines slightly wounded, remained at duty. 2/Lt A.P. Longsdon posted to Y.1.T.M.B. 2/Lt H.R. Jarvis posted to 117 Bty. joined from base.
		4.10 a.m.	Gas which rapidly liberated further North drifted into our lines at Loos and then over DOUBLE CRASSIER.	
		5.30 a.m.	Situation normal. There was a certain amount of artillery fire all day on our trenches and reserve positions. Many working parties were seen.	
	30F	11 a.m. to 4 p.m.	Enemy heavily shelled our front line and were in M5d. About 200 heavy 200lb T.M. bombs being fired and also many 5.9" 4.2" and 77 mm shells.	
		4.30 p.m.	Enemy turned on the area were with 5.9" in M5d. This was considerably thinner his men were seen taken to enemy trenches.	
		10.40 p.m.	Enemy made a raid on HARRISON'S CRATER. Barrage round LENS Rd. G HARRISON'S crater and trenches was immediately put on. This fact and enemy were driven back leaving 3 men killed in our trench. Remainder of day was quiet except for shelling of Loos at intervals.	

C.S.H...... Lt. Col. R.F.A.
Comdg 26 Bde R.F.A.

1st Divisional Artillery

H.Q. 26th BRIGADE R.F.A. ::: M A Y 1916.

Army Form C. 2118

WAR DIARY
or
INTELLIGENCE SUMMARY

(Erase heading not required.)

36 Brigade R.F.A. Vol 12

MAY. 1916

Place	Date	Hour	Summary of Events and Information	Remarks and references to Appendices
LES BREBIS.	May 1		Normal amount of shelling on both battery zones for which the Batteries retaliated in the usual manner.	Reference Maps. Trench Maps. 36 c S.W. 1 Section 6. 36 c S.E. 2 Section 6.
	2.		Quiet day on Battery Zones.	
	3.		Quiet day, slight movement observed in enemy trenches.	
	4.		Enemy more active on the 117th Battery Zone, especially on the S. arm of the DOUBLE CRASSIER and Fosse 5. Also on the 116th Battery's zone enemy artillery was slightly more active than during the past few days. Both batteries carried out usual retaliation. 600s was shelled.	Major A.G. Gu- Canada F.A. fired for 14 days instruction in the trenches
	5.		With the exception of a little shelling of the DOUBLE CRASSIER, a quiet day on both Battery Zones.	
	6.		Normal day on the 116th Battery Zone, on the 117th zone, enemy active with 77m/m gun	
	7.		Normal day on the 116th Zone; the enemy were again active with 77m/m gun on the 117th zone, also with heavy stuff on and near the DOUBLE CRASSIER.	

Army Form C. 2118

WAR DIARY
or
INTELLIGENCE SUMMARY

(Erase heading not required.)

Instructions regarding War Diaries and Intelligence Summaries are contained in F.S. Regs., Part II. and the Staff Manual respectively. Title Pages will be prepared in manuscript.

Place	Date	Hour	Summary of Events and Information	Remarks and references to Appendices
LES BREBIS	May 8.		Normal day. More movement than is usual has been observed during the last few days.	
	9.		Normal.	114th Bty. 1 O.R. wounded remained at duty. 2 O.R. wounded
	10.		Normal.	114th Bty. 1 O.R. slightly wounded, remained at duty, also on the 31st inst. 1 O.R. of 114th Bty was wounded, remained at duty.
	11.		Enemy was more active to-day both on our trenches and rear positions. LES BREBIS was shelled intermittently throughout the day.	
	12.		Quiet day on the whole. Enemy were fairly active with trench mortars on the DOUBLE CRASSIER. LOOS CRASSIER was shelled with 5.9's	
	13.		Normal	
	14.		Normal day in our zone. A certain amount of shelling of LOOS CRASSIER	
	15.		Normal day	
	16.		Normal.	
	17.		Enemy was very active on LOOS & LOOS CRASSIER also trenches on our zone, Batteries retaliated.	On the night of 17/18, the Germans seem to have sent up his lights brown in the sky, presumably for the CHLORINE SECTION from the 3 no...(?)
	18.		Enemy were active in our zone to-day, with various calibre guns & howitzers, also trench mortars.	

Army Form C. 2118

WAR DIARY
or
INTELLIGENCE SUMMARY
(Erase heading not required.)

Instructions regarding War Diaries and Intelligence Summaries are contained in F.S. Regs., Part II. and the Staff Manual respectively. Title Pages will be prepared in manuscript.

Place	Date	Hour	Summary of Events and Information	Remarks and references to Appendices
LES BREBIS	MAY 19.		To-day the enemy were very active & both Battery Zones with various calibre guns, a number of Lachrymatory shells were fired at our rear positions.	The relief were completed on April 7/16 19/19 th. Lt. Col. G.B. HINTON CMG took command of the NEW RIGHT Group.
	20.		Enemy were again very active on the trenches in our Zones, with guns & trench mortars.	POSTINGS. TO 4 Lt. REMPSON G 116 Cpt. J. SASSOON " from B.A.C.
	21.		To-day the enemy bombarded with heavy shells our trenches and our rear position, a number of Lachrymatory shells were fired. This bombardment was simultaneous with a bombardment of our position at the VIMY RIDGE where the Germans made a GAS attack against our trenches, he succeeded in capturing about 15.00 yds.	Lt. RR HOBDAY 6 117 from B.A.C. 2/Lt. Cuerion to BAC from 116 BTY 7/Lt VINER G.A.C from 117 BTY Bdr 116th Bty Corp Lacet 2nd Lt Jones 116 11795 Sgt Lineh 116 11795 became 2nd Lt & to our Rt gd Group
	22.		Enemy activity was normal.	Bdr. J J Ireland A/Cpl 4 Bailey 9/Lt. 43 1300
	23.		The enemy artillery was again very active on our trenches and our rear positions. A barrage was put up by them at various points, this was a second open bombardment preparatory to a counter attack on the ground recently lost on the Vimy RIDGE.	R. M Gream 2/26 Bty of the 16th Bde R.I.A. The 76th B.A.C. became 1st Section of the 1st B.A.C.
	24.		A normal day in our Zones, the enemy however were active in our right.	
	25.		Calonne was heavily shelled otherwise a normal day.	POSTINGS. 2/Lt. TYSON G. 116th Bty.

Army Form C. 2118

WAR DIARY
or
INTELLIGENCE SUMMARY
(Erase heading not required.)

Instructions regarding War Diaries and Intelligence Summaries are contained in F. S. Regs., Part II. and the Staff Manual respectively. Title Pages will be prepared in manuscript.

Place	Date	Hour	Summary of Events and Information	Remarks and references to Appendices
	May 26.		A quiet day.	From the 18th inst. Battery Zones were changed as follows. 117 Bdy. now free from M.21a 3.6.6 M.9.d.2.0. 40th Bdy.
	27.		Enemy's fire was heavy all day both on our trenches and rear positions. Calonne was heavily shelled throughout the day and damage was done to the trenches in front of Calonne. At 10.45 p.m. the enemy attempted a raid on our trenches in this sector preceded by an intense fire from guns of all calibre, however he failed to reach our trenches.	M.20c 4.3.6 M.9.d.8.0. 116th Bdy. (team section) M.10a 7.9.6 Double Canister Inclusive. This section of M.C.
	28.		A quiet day.	Bdy.
	29.		A normal day.	M.20c 4.3 to M.15.c/o.
	30.		Quiet day.	
	31.		Enemy were more active to-day both on our trenches and rear positions. CALONNE was shelled intermittently throughout the day, batteries carried out retaliation as ordered by the Group Commander.	

G.R. Murphy
Lt. Col. RFA
Cdg 26th Bde RFA

1.vi.16

1st Divisional Artillery.

H. Q. 26th BRIGADE R.F.A. ::: JUNE 1916.

Army Form C. 2118

JUNE 1916

WAR DIARY
or
INTELLIGENCE SUMMARY
(Erase heading not required.)

26th Brigade R.F.A.

Vol 23

Place	Date	Hour	Summary of Events and Information	Remarks and references to Appendices
GRENAY R.5.D.9a.10.	JUNE 1.		Enemy was active to-day allround. VIMY RIDGE especially was shelled.	
	2		Quiet day.	
	3.		Except for intermittent trench mortaring of our trenches, a quiet day.	1.O.R wounded of 116 Battery.
	4		Normal	
	5		Enemy rather more active, CALONNE was shelled otherwise a quiet day.	
	6.		Heavy trench mortars active, otherwise a quiet day.	
	7.		CALONNE & our trenches were shelled. Enemy showed himself freely.	
	8.		Normal, a large party of Germans were most suitably dealt with by batteries.	
	9.		Quiet	
	10		Quiet	
	11		Quiet	
	12.		Hostile artillery more active to-day, CALONNE shelled with 77m.m. gun & 4.2 how.	
	13		Quiet day	
	14		Normal	
	15		Quiet; enemy showed himself freely.	

Army Form C. 2118

WAR DIARY
or
INTELLIGENCE SUMMARY
(Erase heading not required.)

Instructions regarding War Diaries and Intelligence Summaries are contained in F. S. Regs., Part II. and the Staff Manual respectively. Title Pages will be prepared in manuscript.

Place	Date	Hour	Summary of Events and Information	Remarks and references to Appendices
GRENAY	JUNE 16		Hostile artillery quiet. Trench mortars rather active.	
	17		Rather more active than during the past few days.	
	18		Enemy trench mortars active all day	
	19		Quiet	
	20		Hostile artillery quiet, trench mortars active.	
	21		Quiet, except for trench mortars, these were fired at and answered. Considerable train activity round LENS.	
	22		Enemy trench mortars much quieter after being "strafed" yesterday.	
	23		Intermittent shelling during the day, trench mortars again active.	
	24		Slight shelling only, trench mortars active	
	25		Trench mortars + 77m guns active all day. The 117th Bty. were employed on wire cutting preparatory to a raid by the 3rd Inf. Bde (Roy. Munster Fus). At night all batteries in the Brigade took part in the intense bombardment preceding and the barrage during, the raid. The raiding party succeeded in entering the enemy trench stayed there 30 minutes,	Raid was on two points vz. M 15 D.4.6 M 15 D.2.1.

WAR DIARY
or
INTELLIGENCE SUMMARY
(Erase heading not required.)

Army Form C. 2118

Place	Date	Hour	Summary of Events and Information	Remarks and references to Appendices
GRENAY	JUNE 25 (CONTD)		The raid was successful in so much that the enemy had many casualties, but no prisoners were brought back as those that were captured had to be despatched as they greatly hampered the removal of our wounded; identifications however were secured. The Brig. Genl. commanding the 3rd Inf. Bde. sent a personal letter of appreciation of the wire cutting & support of the Artillery.	
	26.		Trench mortars & 77m guns active. Our bombardment last night damaged the enemy trenches a lot.	
	27.		Quiet, at 6.p.m. enemy shelled our trenches for about 4 men, 50 rounds fired.	
	28.		Practically no hostile fire.	
	29.		A quiet day except for Trench mortars. 117th cut wire at three points, this was done for the enemy, and part of the general scheme of activity.	
	30.		A quiet day. At 10.p.m. several battery positions were shelled with an 5.9's & 4" guns, this was in retaliation for shelling of enemy trenches. N. of DOUBLE CROSSIER the 2nd Bde. attacked in advance front, Right Group artillery did not co-operate. Civilians apparently employed in the German	

Army Form C. 2118.

WAR DIARY
or
INTELLIGENCE SUMMARY
(Erase heading not required.)

Place	Date	Hour	Summary of Events and Information	Remarks and references to Appendices
GRENAY	JUNE 30 (CONT'D)		Trenches.	
			Summary of the month. The first three weeks normal, with trench mortars on both sides very much in evidence. The last week was marked by the increased activity on the British front.	
			Reference Maps. 36° S.W. Edition 7. 1/10,000 trench map. 36 S.E. 2 " 6 1/10,000	
			C. Betting(?) Lt. Col. R.F.A. Lt. Col. R.F.A. Col¹ 26ᵗʰ Bde R.F.A.	
			1.vii.16	

1st Div.

Headquarters,

26th BRIGADE, R.F.A.

J U L Y

1 9 1 6

1st Divn
Vol 24

Confidential

War Diary
of
26th Brigade R.F.A
from 1st July 1916
to 31st July 1916

Volume 24

Army Form C. 2113.

WAR DIARY
or
INTELLIGENCE SUMMARY

(Erase heading not required.)

JULY 1916

36th Brigade R.F.A.

Instructions regarding War Diaries and Intelligence Summaries are contained in F.S. Regs., Part II. and the Staff Manual respectively. Title Pages will be prepared in manuscript.

Place	Date	Hour	Summary of Events and Information	Remarks and references to Appendices
GRENAY.	July 1.		Nonze day.	Belrup 36 S.W.1
	2.		Orders received regarding relief by 40th Division R.A.	36 S.E.2
	3.		Relief of batteries by 40th B.A. commenced.	
LOZINGHEM	4		Relief completed. "Right Group" was taken over by O.C. 178th Bde R.F.A. 40th R.A. 36 Bde Dn H.Q. Batteries moved by road to LOZINGHEM.	HAZEBROUK 5a 1/100.000
	5-6		Resting at LOZINGHEM.	
HAVERNAS	7.		The Brigade moved by train from LILLERS to CANDAS whence by road to HAVERNAS.	LENS 11 1/100.000
MOLLIENS AU BOIS	8.	9.10 a.m	Marched from HAVERNAS to MOLLIENS-AU-BOIS.	AMIENS 19 1/100.000
	9.10.11		Resting at MOLLIENS-AU-BOIS.	
BEHENCOURT	12		Marched from MOLLIENS-AU-BOIS to BEHENCOURT.	
	13		At BEHENCOURT.	"
Satisfied	14		Marched from BEHENCOURT 11.30 p.m. to bivouac in E.11.B.[?] ALBERT v MOULIN-DE-VIVIER	Sh 62 Sh 162 D 1/40.000
	15.16 17.18		In bivouac E.11.B.	

WAR DIARY or INTELLIGENCE SUMMARY

Army Form C. 2118.

JULY 1916

26 Brigade R.F.A

Place	Date	Hour	Summary of Events and Information	Remarks and references to Appendices
BOTTOM WOOD	July 19		Moved into action. H.Q. at BOTTOM WOOD. Batteries in action in line from a point X.17.c.5.1. to X.23.a.8.6. The 18 pdr batteries i.e 116th & 117th batteries cutting wire on the portion of the German switch line running through S.2.B. This ended in being hung & had to be heavily punching 150 to 300 yds in depth along the front being cut.	Ref/map Sheet 57 D. S.E. Sect. 2 B. 1/20,000
	20 & 21		Wire cutting continued until 4 p.m. and after this occasional rounds on the points cut. The 46th Battery (4.5 howrs) engaged on the German switch line. Enemy artillery active to-day.	
	22			
	23		The 19th Division with the 1st Div. on the left & the 33rd Div. on the right, broke a an attack on the German switch line at 1.30 a.m. This Brigade supported the attack of the 56th Infy Bde 19th Div. whose objective was from S.2.B.8.9. to S.2.a.5.3. The 57th Infy Bde 19 Div. attacked on the immediate right of the 56th Infy Bde. The O.C. 26 Bde R.F.A. was with G.O.C. 56th Infy Bde in BAZENTIN LE PETIT WOOD during operation.	
	24			Ref/map etc.

Army Form C. 2118.

WAR DIARY
or
INTELLIGENCE SUMMARY

(Erase heading not required.)

Instructions regarding War Diaries and Intelligence Summaries are contained in F. S. Regs., Part II. and the Staff Manual respectively. Title Pages will be prepared in manuscript.

Place	Date	Hour	Summary of Events and Information	Remarks and references to Appendices
BOTTOM WOOD	July 25.		Enemy artillery very active (?)	
	26.		Normal amount of shelling during the day. At night the batteries were heavily shelled with gas shells which had the effect of making several officers and men sick and produced unpleasant after-effects.	
	27.		Orders were received at 11.55 p.m. 26th that the 13th & 15th Corps were to attack DELVILLE WOOD & GUILLEMONT today and that the 3rd Corps artillery was to create a diversion by firing on the enemy works opposite 3rd Corps front. This Brigade fired on the German switch line for an hour commencing at 6.10 a.m. from S2a 6.2 to S2 B 6.7. After the hour fire was lifted to MARTIN PUICH, for half an hour, then back to fuel target for 5 minutes and another lift to MARTIN PUICH, then Pam for 5 minutes and ceased. Otherwise a normal day.	Area of MARTIN PUICH
	28.		Normal from 9 p.m. till 5 a.m. 29th but frequent bursts of shrapnel were fired on the German smell (?) line and back to S3 b and a back stands in S3 a (?), the men we to cover when parties were coming up.	"

2449 Wt. W14957/M90 750,000 1/16 J.B.C. & A. Forms/C.2118/12.

Army Form C. 2118.

WAR DIARY
or
INTELLIGENCE SUMMARY

(Erase heading not required.)

JULY 1916

26 Bde R.F.A.

Instructions regarding War Diaries and Intelligence Summaries are contained in F.S. Regs., Part II. and the Staff Manual respectively. Title Pages will be prepared in manuscript.

Place	Date	Hour	Summary of Events and Information	Remarks and references to Appendices
BOTTOM WOOD	July 29.		Artillery activity on both sides. Co-operated in bombardment of the German intermediate line.	Reference Oper. Order
	30.		The 57th D.J Bde 19th Div. attacked the German intermediate line between (S3D4½) S3D0.4 + S2c 8.7 also NEW line between S2D½.6½ + S2c.7.5½. The 76th Bde R.F.A supported this attack by firing on the Switch trench from S2nO.½ to S.2.6.1.6. with one 15 pr battery & one 4.5 how battery also one howitzer batteries with one 18 pdr battery. The 19th Siege Art. were also shooting in support of this attack. the attack took place at 6.10 p.m. At 4 am to 4.30 am this Brigade co-operated in bombardment of intermediate line, on the same regularity as the same hour on previous day.	MARTINPUICH 1/20,000
	31.		Artillery activity otherwise normal day.	

E A Minton
Lt Col
Cdr 26th Bde

July 1916

Army Form C. 2113

WAR DIARY or INTELLIGENCE SUMMARY

26 Divisional R.F.A.

Place	Date	Hour	Summary of Events and Information	Remarks and references to Appendices
	July			
	3		1. O.R. wounded returned at duty. 116th Battery.	
	10		2/Lieut. A.P. ABBOTT posted to 40th Battery from S.R.C.	
	13		2/Lieut J. BLACKBURN 40th Battery posted to ENGLAND	
	14		2/Lieut A.J. BILLINGHURST + S.F. HOPWOOD posted to 40th Battery from S.R.C.	
	19		2/Lieut W.F. FORREST to 116th Bty. 2/Lieut E.C.G. HULL to 117th BTY posted from S.R.C.	
	20		1. O.R. wounded 117th Bty.	
	21		Capt.(temp) F. SASSOON posted to D/S Bty from 116th Bty.	
	21		3 O.R. killed (accidentally) 117th Bty.	
	22		1. O.R. killed 1 O.R. wounded returned at duty 116th Bty. 2 O.R. wounded 40th Bty.	
	24		CAPT.(temp) E.H.P. JACKSON 116th Bty wounded. 1 O.R. killed 2 O.R. wounded 1 O.R. wounded 1 O.R. wounded accident respectively 117/118	
			2 O.R. shell shock 116th Bty. 4 O.R. wounded 1 O.R. wounded 117th Bty.	
	26		CAPT.(temp) S.F. McCONNEL posted to 116th Bty from 117th Bty. 1 O.R. wounded 117th Bty.	
	25		1. O.R. wounded returned at duty H.Q.	
	27		1. O.R. wounded 117th Bty. Killed	
	30		3. O.R. " " 1 B.R. killed 116 Bty. G.B.Murphy Lt. Col	
	31		2 O.R. wounded 117 B.Gy 40 B.G. wounded Oty duty. Cd. 26 F. Bde.	

1st Divisional Artillery

26th BRIGADE

ROYAL FIELD ARTILLERY

AUGUST 1 9 1 6

Vol 25

War Diary
of
26th Brigade R.F.A.
1st to 31st August 1916.
(Volume 25)

WAR DIARY or INTELLIGENCE SUMMARY

Army Form C. 2118.

August 1916. PAGE 1.

26 Brigade R.F.A.

Place	Date	Hour	Summary of Events and Information	Remarks and references to Appendices
BOTTOM WOOD Ref map Sheet 57 D S.E. ED. 2.B. Square X.29.	August 1.		The Brigade took no part in any operations.	[M]
	2.		Batteries carried out bombardments commencing at 3 p.m. Zones allotted as follows. 116th Group between S.20.9.4. to S.28.1½.4½.* and S.21.D.2.4. to S.27.D.4.4.# 117th Group between S.21.b.6.2. to 9.4.; S.22.c.8.4. to S.21.D.2.4. to S.26.1½.4.½. front of SWITCH LINE S.22.a.6.2. to S.26.1½.4.½.	*Trench farm Ref map AREA of MARTIN PUICH ED. B. [A]
	3.		The bombardment was repeated at 5 a.m. It should also have been carried out at the 4.5"s & 6" inch preparatory to an attack on the SWITCH LINE but was cancelled for these this day. In preparation for an attack on the INTERMEDIATE LINE the 40th (how) battery bombarded this line from 12 noon to 2 p.m. between S.2.D.7.5 and S.2.C.8.4.	
	4.		The 34th Division attacked the INTERMEDIATE LINE between S.2.C.8.4 and S.3.C.0.5. at 1.10 a.m. Batteries fired as follows from "C" 60 secs to 0.30 secs. 116th INTER. LINE S.2.D.0.4. to S.2.D.2.4½. 117th Bty. S.2.C.8.4. to S.2.D.0.4. for 15 secs of this time fire was directed on NO MANS LAND in front of enemy [trench] from +0.30 to +0.10 mins fire lifted 50 yards over INTER. LINE onwards	

AUGUST 1916.   PAGE 2

Army Form C. 2118.

WAR DIARY
or
INTELLIGENCE SUMMARY
(Erase heading not required.)

26 Brigade R.F.A.

Place	Date	Hour	Summary of Events and Information	Remarks and references to Appendices
BOTTOM WOOD	August 4 (cont)		(how) Bty fired on barricades at S2a7.2 and S2c8.8. from 0-60 mins. The 40 (how) Bty fired on barricades at S2a7.2 and S2c8.8. from 0-60 mins. to 40-60 minutes. At the request of G.O.C. 101st Inf. Bde the barrage was continued for about an hour and a half. The enemy let off gas the night 3/4 inst. on our left, but no eno attack. From 9 p.m. to 1 a.m. 4th inst 116 & 117th Bty fired salvoes every 15 mins. on the exits from MARTINPUICH at M32a2.6. M32a8.7. M132c24. and M32c4.6. 3 guns each (2 guns only). In conjunction with an attack by ANZAC to be made by the 2nd Division whenever to establish themselves in MUNSTER ALLEY, the 101st Inf. Bde attacked the INTER LINE NE. of POZIERES at 9.15 p.m. and by the 23rd Division to apprehend at 11 p.m. previous to this bombing parties made any from tank flanks. This Brigade was ordered to be prepared to open fire if called on, behind the INTER LINE. The Batteries fired a barrage from 4.0 p.m. to 0 low 1.30 a.m. The aiming line behind the Sperberry thread : S2Ba0. S2Bc0. S2c7.6. S2c72.62. which was the front attacked from alow S2a7.6. S2c87. S2c72.62.	MARS MEEQG MARTINPUICH

AUGUST 1916.

PAGE 3.

Army Form C. 2118.

WAR DIARY
or
INTELLIGENCE SUMMARY

(Erase heading not required.)

76 Brigade R.F.A.

Place	Date	Hour	Summary of Events and Information	Remarks and references to Appendices
BOTTOM WOOD	4th Aug	5.	O.C. 76th Brigade R.F.A. was sent the G.O.C 101st Inf. Bde during the operation. In order to relate the portion of the INTER. LINE held by the enemy 116th & 117th Batteries fired on salvo per battery every ten minutes 4 p.m. to 10 p.m. on zones as follows 116th road in S20 (inclusive) to S20.7½ 117th road in S20 (inclusive) to road in S20 (inclusive) both batteries 150 yds and INTER. LINE and raked bach to SWITCH LINE between S20.6.2 and S20.6.7. The 101st Inf. Bde again attacked the INTER. LINE at 11.30 p.m. Targets of batteries were the same as last night (4th inst.) i.e. 40th Bty. communication trench S2a-c from barricade S2c.7.86 SWITCH LINE. 116th Barrage from barricade S20.4.9. (gun on road) to S20.8. 117th Barrage from S20.1.8. to S20.7.8 (barricade) fire was opened at 11.30 p.m. and ceased at 1.30 a.m. 6 Min. B.C. 76th Batteries with L.O.C. 101st Inf. Bde. R.H.	A.1
		6.	The firing for the purpose of locating the INTER LINE was repeated to-day from 7 a.m. to 2 p.m. To test the method of synchronizing watches	

Army Form C. 2118.

WAR DIARY
or
INTELLIGENCE SUMMARY

(Erase heading not required.)

AUGUST 1916.   PAGE 4.

26th Brigade R.F.A.

Place	Date	Hour	Summary of Events and Information	Remarks and references to Appendices
BOTTOM WOOD.	August 6 (con)		heaps of lights dropped from an aeroplane at about 9 or so for hours, & the III Corps was fired at times which would show all the shells arriving at 6.30 p.m. in the German lines, an aeroplane dropped lights at 6, 5, 6.15 & 6.15 p.m. and the shells were fired each battery (taking its approximate line of flight of projectile) the burst from M.17 06 i 2 — M.33 D i 1. was helping to from the INTERMEDIATE	5.15 pm — 6 pm by the Brigade. from 10.30 pm 6.35 pm Airman (shown) [illeg] airman (from official) M.17 0 i 5 M.33 D i 1. [illeg] Ref.
	7.		The 11th Northumberland Fusiliers attacked the "Elbow" of the INTERMEDIATE LINE at about S.2.c.8.4. at 8.30 a.m. the 116th & 117th Bdes, the INTER LINE barraged as follows 116th Bdy. S.2.D.4½.7. to S.2.D.7.6. 117th Bdy. S.2.D.4½.7. to 75.N.W. of road at S.2.D.3½.6. fire was kept up from 8.31 am to 9.31 am. 39th Bde R.F.A. barraged the SWITCH LINE from S.2.a.6.1. to 250 x 6 N.E. of "Dead Sous" and fired at 5.15 pm. march to attack the INTER	[illeg]
	8.		Enemy artillery active today. Batteries continued to attack the INTER LINE from 3.0 am to 5.0 am, 9.0 am to 10.0 am, and 4.0 pm to 8.30 pm. also between 2.0 am and 4.0 am the approach to the SWITCH LINE. In conjunction with a bombardment by heavy artillery from 4.0 am to 6.0 am	

Army Form C. 2118.

PAGE 5.

WAR DIARY
or
INTELLIGENCE SUMMARY

(Erase heading not required.)

26th Bde R.F.A.

AUGUST 1916.

Place	Date	Hour	Summary of Events and Information	Remarks and references to Appendices
BOTTOM WOOD	August 8.		The 117th Battery bombarded MARTINPUICH in M.32.c. This was in addition to the shooting mentioned before during the hours 4.0 am to 5 am. At 9.30 pm the 112th Inf. Bde pushed forward along officers patrols with a view to occupying the portion of the intermediate line held by the Germans; in support of this operation the 40th (how) Bty bombarded the intermediate line from 5.20 to 7.30 pm; from 7.30 to 9.30 pm. Odd rounds were fired into the INTER. line; from 8.30 pm to 9.40 pm a barrage was put up for 50 yards on either side of the end running N. + S. though S.2.a. and e between on batty of 18 pdrs fired this and searched 150 yards over INTER line and SWITCH LINE at batty fire 15 secs; the barrage was made intense from 9.40 pm to 10.0 pm. The Bde were for this also from road (inc) in S.2.a + c to road (exc) in S.2.b + d; after 10.0 pm AM this gradually slowed down cease ceased.	
	9.		With a view to completely destroying the Intermediate line to the SW of the 1st + 15th D.A. bombarded it during the hours of daylight, the	

WAR DIARY or INTELLIGENCE SUMMARY

Army Form C. 2118.
AUGUST 1916. PAGE 6.

26th Brigade R.??

Place	Date	Hour	Summary of Events and Information	Remarks and references to Appendices
BOTTOM WOOD	August 9 (contd)		40th (How.Bty) bombarded between the elbow S2.c.8.4. and sunken line between S2.c + S2.d. An occasional round on road & communication trench in S2.a.c. Isolation barrage was continued, this is done in conjunction with the 15th D.A. batteries of the 15th Jat R.A. taking turns of duty.	
			open programme.	
	10/11		Isolation barrage continued. The Royce M.G. harass 112 Inf. Bde. made a bombing attack on the Intermediate line tonight at 2 a.m. 116th fired from S2.o.15.5 ½ to S2.o.o.5. and the 117th Bg from road (incl.) to S2.B.6-S2.o.0.5. Isolation barrage continued during the 11th inst.	
	12		Isolation barrage continued, attention was paid to works about MARTINPUICH. 2 gns.S.I.(?/13) in conjunction with an attack by the 4th Australian Div. to the S. and E. of MOUQUET FARM and one by the 15th Bde. on the SWITCH LINE from about S.10.9.9. to X.a.4. in MUNSTER ALLEY. The 119th Inf Bde attacked that portion of Intermediate line that	

WAR DIARY

AUGUST 1916 PAGE 7.

26th Brigade R.F.A.

Place	Date	Hour	Summary of Events and Information	Remarks and references to Appendices
BOTTOM WOOD.	August 12th (cont)		fired by the enemy i.e. from about S2c8.5 to S2D 4.6. Preparatory to this the isolation barrage was continued till zero hour 10.30 p.m. 13th inst. from Noon to 3 p.m. heavy Artillery bombarded the INTER LINE from S2.0.0.5. to S2c8.8. And the communication trench running N from S2c8.5 to S2C8.8. from 3.0 p.m to 8.0 p.m 40" (how) Bty fired one round per two minutes on target above (Munic). Its how Bty of 39th Bde fired from Noon to 8.0 p.m. on the INTER LINE from S20.0.5. to S20 3.6. the 117th Bty fired bursts on the Inter line opposite Bde line, for 3 secs from Zero Cue 18pcs of 26" + 39" Bdes fired n.b No ABMS land. 76" Section S2c 8.5. to S2D.O.S. from her 1st + 3 min life n.b objective. and the entered for certain Barrage 150s on the objective. O.C. 76th Bar R.F.A. was with L.O.E. 117th Inf. Bde. RW during the operations. Col Inskety required a slow rate of fire on reports from + 1 hour hits 2.15 a.m. 13th inst.	
	13th		Isolation barrage continued. This Brigade took no part in any operations. RW	

AUGUST 1916. Page 8.

WAR DIARY
or
INTELLIGENCE SUMMARY
(Erase heading not required.)

Army Form C. 2118.

26th Brigade R.F.A.

Place	Date	Hour	Summary of Events and Information	Remarks and references to Appendices
BOTTOM WOOD	August 14.		The Brigade took no part in any operation. New barrages (notation) were fired in place of those mentioned previously, known as barrage E.F.&G. area was from MARTIN POICH (including works thereabouts) to SWITCHING TRENCH	RM
	15.		No operation on our front.	RM
	16.		A bombardment of the INTERMEDIATE LINE from ELBOW (S.20.B.5.5.) to point S.20.O.5. This was in preparation for an attack on the 18th inst. by the 1st Brigade (Inf.). This was a Chinese attack at 7.20 p.m. to-day. The 1st & 3rd Inf. Bdes made an attack on the ENTER LINE from S.30.4.8.6 and S.30. and S.20.7.4.9. They did not require a barrage. S.O.S. called to read S.20.7.4.9. The whole isolation barrage was fired using much times each batteries were engaged on bombardments preparatory to the attack to-morrow inst.	RM
	17.		Chinese attack at 1.30 p.m. Preparatory to attack to-morrow 18 inst. The isolation barrages were carried out by batteries of 1st & 5th R.A. the 4 & 5 how. Bty. of same B.A.'s bombarded parker roads in M.33.c. Orchards So of A Res track from N.W. corner of HIGH WOOD through S.3 on two	RM

AUGUST 1916.   PAGE 9.

Army Form C. 2118.

26th Brigade R.F.A

WAR DIARY
or
INTELLIGENCE SUMMARY
(Erase heading not required.)

Place	Date	Hour	Summary of Events and Information	Remarks and references to Appendices
BOTTOM WOOD.	August 17.		The 40th (How Bty 36 Bde) fired on Sunken roads in S7a - S7b and trenches in M32c, S1E & M37D S.W.	104
	18.		In preparation for an attack the Intermediate line was bombarded by our batteries from the ELBOW (about S7e 8.9.) to S7.0.0-5. The 39th Bde carried on from this point to S7D 45.6. The intermediate barrage was also continued. An attack by 1st Division attacked the Intermediate line at 4.15 a.m. supported by the 39th Bde R.F.A. Zone as follows: 76th S7e 6.5.6. to 5. 39th S7 D.0-5. to 37.6.5 (when track crosses road) The 2nd Inf Bde attacked the new German trench from the track about S3 & 48. to its western extremity about S3 e 6.9. An attack on an extra front from S2e - Chiark, HIGHWOOD was launched at 2.30 p.m. to-day, from S2e - Chiark, HIGHWOOD and to the S.E. of it, in preparation for this the Objective was bombed from 5pm 16th inst until 3.00 18th inst meaning of course to harass of SWITCH LINE; a similar attack took place at 1.30 p.m. B.E.F. 2nd Bde R.F.A. was much "G.O.C. 1st Bde. R.F. during operations	104

AUGUST 1916. PAGE 10.

Army Form C. 2118.

WAR DIARY
or
INTELLIGENCE SUMMARY

(Erase heading not required.) 26th Brigade G.F.3

Place	Date	Hour	Summary of Events and Information	Remarks and references to Appendices
BOTTOM WOOD	August 19.		The usual isolation barrage was continued. No operations.	Nil
	20.		The Bde took no part in any operation. The usual barrages were carried out. The area was bombarded to relieve the SWITCH LINE (Helano) and INTERMEDIATE LINE between Ferndoires & N road (between) S2 & E. Brincing two groves S2 & S3. The 36 Bde took turns with the 76th Bde in firing this barrage. 1. 18pr - 1 4.5" how manned by each Bde.	Nil
	21.		Isolation barrage continued. In conjunction with attack by 14th & 15th Corps and discharge of smoke by 15th Division the 76th Bde R.F.A fired on follows 40 R Bty (4.5 how) 3.30 to 4.30 pm Bde R.F.A. fired as follows. Intermediate line from road in deliberate bombardment of Intermediate line from road in S7-D6 150x East of road in ELBOW at S7c 8.9. 116th + 117th Btys fired from 4.38 to 4.30 pm on SWITCH LINE. At 4.30. artillery barrage lifted 200x N. for 2min. then fired 2nds per pm on original objective.	Nil
	22.		The Bde took no part in any operation. Barrage continued.	Nil

WAR DIARY or INTELLIGENCE SUMMARY

AUGUST 1916   PAGE 11   26 Brigade R.F.A.

Army Form C. 2118.

Place	Date	Hour	Summary of Events and Information	Remarks and references to Appendices
BOTTOM WOOD	August 23.		Barrage was kept up during the night including new trenches though M33a & c. a M33a & M33D.	R.A.
	24.		At stated times to operation in which we were chiefly engaged. At 5.45 p.m. the Inchape Minnie Tuicies attacked the Intermediate line by bombing from both flanks, simultaneously the 15th Division seized the Northern end of new trench at about S7 c 9.9. and bombed down it, the 33rd Division attacked TEA TRENCH (S.11). The programme of action of this Brigade was as follows; barrages were dropped two hours before Zero. Zero - 2 hours to zero the 40th (How) Bty bombarded S7 D1.5½ = NEW ELBOW to road at S7 D 3½. 6½ inclusive also the 117th Bty, 116th scorched comm trench from NEW ELBOW for 150 yards to North. Zero Zero to + 1 hour 40th (How) Bty 150 yards over offensive keeping all fire clear N/ & at 150 yards to EAST of comm trench running from S7a S7 D. /c NEW ELBOW. 117th Bty Sunken road about S7 B 2.5½. 116th left and sunken rectangle S7 B 5.0 - 5.10 - 10.10 - 10.0. 15th & 47th D.A. whom is also barraged various enemy works & gun positions.	Ref map 1/10,000 photograph lined corrected to 22/8/16. R.A.

AUGUST 1916   PAGE 12

Army Form C. 2118.

WAR DIARY
or
INTELLIGENCE SUMMARY

(Erase heading not required.)

26th Brigade R.F.A.

Place	Date	Hour	Summary of Events and Information	Remarks and references to Appendices
BOTTOM WOOD	August 25.		During the night 24/25 inst. the 116 & 117th fired on the enemy works around MARTINPUICH. At 11.30 p.m. the 3rd Inf. Bde. attacked the Intermediate line the 26th Bde R.F.A. co-operated by firing on the objective from road (inclusive) S.20.b.5.0 to S.9.a.4 (inclusive) to an hour, also the comm't trench S.23.b.6 to S.23.c.9.9. The fire was prepared, each covering party moved to its own area. The above bombardment was continued. At 7-30 the attack was prepared, each covering party moved to its own. The attacks of the 24th inst. were very successful. Several hundred prisoners including about 20 officers were captured & much ground gained including the remainder of DELVILLE WOOD. Enemy artillery active & trenches.	RM
	26.		A further attack on the Intermediate line as at 6 p.m. resulted in 300 yards of the trench being gained, the Brigade fired each gun as a fr previous attacks, fire however was kept up till 6.30 a.m. 27th inst. Enemy infantry very quiet.	RM

WAR DIARY or INTELLIGENCE SUMMARY

Army Form C. 2118.

AUGUST 1916   PAGE 13.

26 Brigade R.F.A.

Place	Date	Hour	Summary of Events and Information	Remarks and references to Appendices
BOTTOM WOOD	August 27		The 1st Division took over the line from the 15th Division on our right. The boundaries of the 1st Division are now on the right:- MACGREGOR TRENCH (about S.10.B.8.4) on the left:- S.3.0.7.5. Telephone lines were all down were picked up by 6am. to-day but batteries were prepared to fire if required on the SOS registration. This Brigade was not responsible for any particular part of the line but batteries registered on WOOD LANE and the trenches at the N.W. corner of HIGH WOOD. The Brigade supplied a liaison officer with 1st Bde H.Q. Inf. Today. Batteries were laid on SWITCH LINE from S.4.B.0.3. to S.5 Central. Their particular attention was paid to the registration of WOOD LANE.	
	28.		Registration & reduction of gun pits was continued. Enemy artillery active. Proposed attack on the 29th inst. postponed. High firing by our [illegible] across the Short discharge by 1st-15th Divs. at 7 p.m. Batteries did not fire.	
	29.		The Bosch from M.34.D.2.O. to M.35.a.0.5 was searched during [illegible]	

AUGUST 1916.   PAGE 14.   Army Form C. 2118.

WAR DIARY
or
INTELLIGENCE SUMMARY
(Erase heading not required.)

26th Brigade R.F.A.

Place	Date	Hour	Summary of Events and Information	Remarks and references to Appendices
BOTTOM WOOD	(August) 30.		Shelling of importance on our front, the day was very wet & and the mud churned up catapulted things a lot. The German who had INTERMEDIATE LINE (man late 3a) announced, Jefferis & 90 men carrier, she had much just recently had an effect on them apparently.	
	31.		The enemy started a barrage at 9 a.m. roughly on the ground referred to in Squares 51 to 21 also on our Battery positions and MAMETZ WOOD, he made feints of Shrapnel lock "bar" & otherwise, at about 3 p.m. he attacked TEA TRENCH held by 24th Div. (on our right) & light trench map No. reference. He captured the trench from a point where it meets WOOD LANE to a point short from PEACH TRENCH and also he advanced certain portions of ORCHARD TRENCH. The 111th Bty were shelled well & rather all night (31/7/16). The Brigade opened fire in support of the 24th Division and returned his 9-30 p.m. The attack by	

AUGUST 1916. PAGE 15

Army Form C. 2118.

WAR DIARY
or
INTELLIGENCE SUMMARY

(Erase heading not required.)

26 Brigade R.F.A.

Place	Date	Hour	Summary of Events and Information	Remarks and references to Appendices
BOTTOM WOOD.	August 31.		the 1st Division due to take place on the 1st Sept was postponed. Night firing by batteries as for 30th.	
			Reference Maps: 1. Quad of MARTIN PUICH	
			2. Sheet 57c S.W. Edn 2.D	
			3. " 57D S.E. " 2.B	
			4. Various lithograph maps issued by CORPS from time to time.	

L. K. Minchin
Lt. Col. R.F.A.
O/c 26th Bde R.F.A.

1.4.16

AUGUST 1916 PAGE 16

Army Form C. 2118.

WAR DIARY
or
INTELLIGENCE SUMMARY

(Erase heading not required.)

26 Brigade A.F.A.

Place	Date	Hour	Summary of Events and Information	Remarks and references to Appendices
BOTTOM WOOD	August		Casualties & Postings.	
	1.		One O.R. (40th) wounded	
	2.		" O.R. (117th) "	
	6.		O.R. (40th) wounded (remained at duty) 1. O.R. (40th) to Hospital Shellshock	
			O.R. (117) wounded	
	9.		" 116 "	
			" (40th) to Hospital Shell Shock	
	11		2 O.R. killed, 3 O.R. wounded (40th). 1 O.R. (116) wounded remained at duty.	
	17.		Lt. R. EMPSON wounded (to England) 1 O.R. killed (116th)	
	19.		One O.R. (116) wounded remained at duty.	
	27.		2 O.R. (40) killed, 4 O.R. (40th) 3 O.R. (116) wounded.	
	31.		2/Lt. E.C.G. NULL wounded. 1 O.R. killed. 18 O.R. wounded (including 2 N.C.O.)	
	25.		2/Lt. W.H. M'Combie to 116th Bty.	
	30.		" S.D.S. Jones " 117th "	
	31.		2/Lt. E.A. RYRIE " 116th " Lt. G.E. SAMUELS to 40th Bty	

1st Divisional Artillery.

H. Q. 26th BRIGADE R.F.A. ::: SEPTEMBER 1916.

SEPTEMBER 1916.   PAGE 1.

Army Form C. 2118.

WAR DIARY
or
INTELLIGENCE SUMMARY.
(Erase heading not required.)

26th Brigade R.F.A.

Hour, Date, Place	Summary of Events and Information	Remarks and references to Appendices
SEPT.		
BOTTOM WOOD. 1.	The 24th Division counter-attacked TEA-TRENCH (captured by the enemy on the 31st August) at 6.30 p.m. This Brigade co-operated by shooting on WOOD LANE as follows. 40th (How) Bty. Junction of comm" trenches at ELBOW SA.D.5.6. 116th Bty. SA.D.6.5.6. SA.D.5.6., 117th Bty. SA.D.5.6.6. when WOODLANE enters HIGH WOOD; fire opened at once at 6.30 p.m. to 6.50 p.m. (4 rounds a gun a minute) and decreased to B.F. 1 min. until 8.30 p.m. at request of Infantry. Fire was maintained for some time after this.	REF. MAPS. 1/ AREA OF MARTINPUICH 1/10,000 lithograph map issued by III Corps. 2/ TRENCH MAP. FRANCE SHEET. 57D S.E. EDN. 2B.
X.29.a. SHEET. 57D S.E. EDTN 2B.		
2.	A discharge of smoke by the 1st & 15th Divisions. As a preliminary to the attack by the 4th ARMY on the 3rd inst. the heavies bombarded WOODLANE AND NORTHERN portion of HIGH WOOD, also this Brigade systematically searched vicinity of the objectives as follows from 8 a.m. 2nd inst till Zero 3rd inst., 40th Bty. comm" trench running	

WAR DIARY or INTELLIGENCE SUMMARY

(Erase heading not required.)

Army Form C. 2118.

PAGE 2.

Hour, Date, Place	Summary of Events and Information	Remarks and references to Appendices

1 (contd) EAST from S.4.d.5½.6.½ for 360 yards also the 90th Bty to operate with the 116th & 117th Btys whose targets were — to search at irregular intervals the area between WOOD LANE (inc) and a line 700 yards N of SWITCH LINE between S.5.c.0.0. to S.5.a 5.0. and the line of com. trench (inc.) S.4.d.5½.7. to S.5.a 1.3. the 116th 117th also fired at the targets engaged by the heavies to prevent the enemy working them.

A most unfortunate incident has to be recorded to-day — a shell struck and destroyed a dug-out in the 117th Bty position, CAPT. M.H. PROUDFOOT R.A.M.C. medical officer attached to the Brigade, 2/Lt. T.S. SPENCER & 2/Lt. S.D.S. JONES A 117th Bty, were killed, and CAPT. H.N. FAIRBANK O/C 117th Bty, was wounded and sent to hospital, other ranks casualties were 1 OR. killed & 2 OR wounded were caused by the shell.

117th position is near ACID DROP COPSE at map 57] S.E. EDTN. 2.B.

Army Form C. 2118.

WAR DIARY
or
INTELLIGENCE SUMMARY.
(Erase heading not required.)

Hour, Date, Place	Summary of Events and Information	Remarks and references to Appendices
Sept. 3.	The preliminary bombardments were continued until Zero hour which was 12 noon. Smoke accompanied by artillery fire was released at 5 a.m. The 4th Army attacked in conjunction with the FRENCH. XVth CORPS attacked GINCHY and ground E. of DELVILLE WOOD. The 1st Inf. Bde attacked German front line from the point S16 B 9½ 8 to where it strikes the wedge of HIGH WOOD at S3 D 9.8. The attack in the WOOD was assisted by various appliances - FLAMMEN WERFERS etc. The 47th D.A. took part in the preliminary bombardment. There was no increase in the intensity of the fire either of heavy or field artillery up to Zero. H.O.C. 26th Bde R.F.A. acted as Artillery adviser to the G.O.C. 1st Inf. Bde at the H.Q. at BAZENTIN LE GRAND. The Brigades co-operated as follows: - 90 m.m. to Zero 90 (Note) (Lacs) Bly common trench from S9D 7.8½. to function with	Note: Ref. map. 1/5,000 lithograph 390 - 291. and sheet 1/96. Compiled from air photo 221

PAGE A.

Army Form C. 2118.

WAR DIARY
or
INTELLIGENCE SUMMARY.
(Erase heading not required.)

Hour, Date, Place	Summary of Events and Information	Remarks and references to Appendices
Sept 3 (contd)	with SWITCH LINE at S5a 33. 116th & 117th Btys searched carefully, area between WOOD LANE and SWITCH LINE between a line S5c 0.0. to S5a 5.0. and a line parallel to it through S5a 0.0. from 0.0. to 0.60 minutes 90ᵒ (hour) B.Cy. searched rectangle from SWITCH LINE (incl) between S5a 2½.3. and S5a 6.2 to a line S5 a.0.0. - S5c 2.8. At +30 minutes and blue 1 hour on action fired 35 rounds of P.S. shell into SUNKEN ROAD in S9B where it crossed SWITCH LINE. 116th Bty fired on WOOD LANE from S9D 7.3½ to ELBOW S9D 5½.6½ and raked back 300 yards. 117th Bty German trench from junction between with WOOD LANE at S9D 5½.6½ to 108 yards WEST and raked back to a line S9B 1.1½ - S9 a 6.0. A barrage was kept up for some time after ds afforded. 60 minutes after Zero. M.G.'s firing by batteries in the vicinity of above targets.	

WAR DIARY
or
INTELLIGENCE SUMMARY

PAGE 5.

Hour, Date, Place	Summary of Events and Information	Remarks and references to Appendices
SEPT. 4.	HIGH WOOD was heavily bombarded by all calibre heavy artillery. The relief of this Brigade by the 39th Bde R.F.A. was commenced, one section of each battery being relieved and proceeding to wagon lines at F.8.a	Kuba a CHINESE ATTACK to-day, followed by infantry fire on WOOD LANE and vicinity.
5.	Relief completed, the Liaison officer from 26 Bde R.F.A. at Inf Bde H.Q. was relieved by an officer of 39th Bde R.F.A. H.Q. moved to wagon line F.8.a	
6.		
11.	Battery at wagon lines. On the 9th inst. a party of 1 Officer and 50 O.R. proceeded to MULT Road Camp for seven days.	
12.	The Brigade moved out of the forward area to BEHENCOURT, to rest.	
30.	BEHENCOURT.	

Wagon line
F.8.a.
1/40,000
SHEET. 62 D.
BEHENCOURT.
as map above.

Army Form C. 2118.

PAGE 6.

WAR DIARY
or
INTELLIGENCE SUMMARY.
(Erase heading not required.)

Hour, Date, Place	Summary of Events and Information	Remarks and references to Appendices
SEPT.	Casualties Sept. 1916.	
1.	1 O.R. 117 Bty. 10 O.R. 90th Bty. wounded.	
2.	Capt. H.H. Proudfoot 90 Bde. 2/Lt. J.S. Spencer	
	2/Lt. S.D.S. Jones killed. 1. O.R. 117 killed.	
	Capt. H.N. Fairbank, 3 O.R. 117 Bty. and 1 O.R.	
	116 Bty wounded. Postings Sept 1916.	
2.	Lt. V.C. Miditch to temp command 117 Bty. Lt. C.R. Reckitt (R.N.M. force)	
3.	2/Lts R.C. Knowles, E.M. Wilkins + R. Alexander to 117 Bty from 1st R.H.C.	
15.	Lt. E.J. Driscoll 117 Bty. to 115th Bty. D.S. Bde.	
16.	Capt. H.N. Fairbank rejoined from Base hospital. Lt. H.E. McInce to 116 Bty from 1 S.T.C.	
17.	2/Lt. A.J. Billinghurst 90th Bty. to 1st R.B.C.	
31.	Lt. H.E. McInce 116 Bty. to 23rd R.S.A. 2/Lt. R.C. Knowles French mortar course	
30.	Lt. G.C. Taylor R.V.C. posted.	

G. Smyth
Lt. Col. R.G.A.
Comg. 35th Bde. R.G.A.

1st Divisional Artillery.

H. Q. 26th BRIGADE R.F.A. ::: OCTOBER 1916.

OCTOBER ~~NOVEMBER~~ 1916.

Army Form C. 2118.

WAR DIARY
or
INTELLIGENCE SUMMARY.
(Erase heading not required.)

PAGE 1

26th Brigade R.F.A.

Instructions regarding War Diaries and Intelligence Summaries are contained in F. S. Regs., Part II. and the Staff Manual respectively. Title pages will be prepared in manuscript.

Hour, Date, Place	Summary of Events and Information	Remarks and references to Appendices
BEHENCOURT. Oct 1/ Sheet 62D Y.20.000 1st EDN. C19a.	Resting at BEHENCOURT, a warning order was received on the night of the 7/8th inst., that the Brigade less one battery would go into action on the 8th inst.	
8.	The Brigade less the 116th Battery proceeded from BEHENCOURT to take up positions in the line under the command of the C.R.A. 47th Division. The Brigade H.Q. when on its march were ordered to return to BEHENCOURT, the 40th (How) & 117th Bty. marched to their wagon lines at BOTTOM WOOD about X.29a. (ref. map. SHEET 57D SE. EDN 23 1/20.000) and stayed there during the night 8/9 inst.	
9.	40th Bty. A position for one section was selected in STAR-FISH TRENCH at M.34.D.8.7. (area of MARTINPUICH EDN B 1/20.000) this position in the open about 1 foot of cover only. 117 removed to wagon lines.	
10.	40th Bty. Worked on new position, gave in orders at 1.10 p.m.	B.O.R. arrived at 117th Bty

WAR DIARY or INTELLIGENCE SUMMARY

Army Form C. 2118.
PAGE 2

Hour, Date, Place	Summary of Events and Information	Remarks and references to Appendices
Oct 10 (cont.)	117th Bty. Several shots over from C/35 Bty R.F.A.(T) in M.36.a.1-3. (ref. 57 C S.W. 20,000) at 10.30 a.m firing on M.17-18. 90th Bty under command of 237th Bde R.F.A.(T) 47th Division to see with the section on the BUTTE DE WARLENCOURT. wagon lines shifted to Sqd 6.6 An old gun position gave 8 good shelters for men and fair standing for horses. 117th Bty were firing a retire sat for the attack by the 9th Division on the 13th and with GIRD LINE, SUPPORT & the BUTTE.	
12	90th Bty received orders for attack on SNAG TRENCH, acting C.O.R. wounded 117 Bty to fire a creeping barrage. The attack was also to contain success. The 117th prepared for and supported the left of the attack. The 9th C.D.A relieved 47th D.A. 90th under the 50th Bde R.F.A and 117th under 52nd Bde R.F.A of the 9th Division.	
13	90th continued work on O.P.s and gun position NEW O.P. at LE SARS (AREA OF MARTINPUICH)	2/Lieut R. H. JARVIS 117th Bty wounded

WAR DIARY
or
INTELLIGENCE SUMMARY.

Army Form C. 2118.

PAGE 3.

Hour, Date, Place	Summary of Events and Information	Remarks and references to Appendices
Oct 13 (con't)	The attack yesterday was known to have failed, our infantry had retired to our front line. Enemy artillery very active on the front of the 117th Bty during the morning & afternoon becoming intense at 5.0 p.m. Our infantry sent up S.O.S rockets and the 117th opened fire at 6.30 p.m enemy fire slackened, 117th ceased. The actual relief of the 235 Bde by the 53rd Bde not passed 6.0 p.m registration checked during the morning.	
14	40th Bty registered from new O.P. this laid to LEFT BTTN 117th Bty right firing 1-3 am between front Y GIRD LINES 40th continued wire & gun positions. 117th participated in a few small tentatives of enemy's system at 1.0 p.m and 8.45 p.m. Officers thousand the day with 5.9.0	
15	The 40th Bty came under the command of the 75th Bde R.F.A fired 150 per gun on SNAG TRENCH	1.O.B a number 117 Bty.

WAR DIARY
or
INTELLIGENCE SUMMARY.

(Erase heading not required.)

Army Form C. 2118.

PAGE 4

Hour, Date, Place	Summary of Events and Information	Remarks and references to Appendices
Oct 16 (cont)	117th Bty bombarded enemy's line M17d 3.5 during the day (50 rounds per gun H.E.) Bty was shelled with 5.9" gas shell during the evening.	
17	90th opened fire with 30th Bty (how) in MORTIMPUICH the was preparing to attack the enemy's dump position, fired 100 rounds per gun on TAIL TRENCH. 117th bombarded enemy line at and about M17d 3.5 during the day (150 rounds per gun H.E.) rehearsal of attack bombardment at 4.0 p.m. S.O.S. was at 7.0 p.m. The 116th Bty marched from BEHENCOURT to relieve the 113th Bty the relief was known to be finished for 24 hours. 116th stayed at wagon lines for night 17/18 inst.	1. O. R. wounded 117th Bty.
18	90th Bty fired a creeping barrage in support of attack at 3.40 a.m. and continued till 8 a.m. The attack was successful except a left and of right near the station of the German M.Guns unable to fire at 3.30 a.m.	

WAR DIARY or INTELLIGENCE SUMMARY.

(Erase heading not required.)

Army Form C. 2118.

PAGE 5.

Hour, Date, Place	Summary of Events and Information	Remarks and references to Appendices
Oct. 18 (cont)	infantry occupied the whole of their objective SNAG TRENCH. A German counter attack at 7 a.m. was soon driven off. 117th Bty (new sheford by our own time) this attack failed. SNAG TRENCH now taken by the 26th Inf Bde 9th Divn. One section 116th Bty relieved one section of the 113th Bty & action close to the road 300 yards WEST OF HIGH WOOD (S.3 & 8.A.½) (AREA OF MARTINPUICH).	
19.	10th Bty took over from 30th Bty in MARTINPUICH at 7.45 a.m. the section in action having been withdrawn to wagon lines during the night 18/19 inst, under the 59th Bde R.F.A. covering the Right Bttn 9th Division situated on BUTTE, fired on S.O.S. lines several times during the night the 117th also fired S.O.S. line 116th registered TAIL TRENCH and Zero line. 20. 90th registered from CRESCENT ALLEY O.P. SNAG TRENCH was reconnoitred for O.P.s but without avail.

WAR DIARY
or
INTELLIGENCE SUMMARY.

(Erase heading not required.)

Army Form C. 2118.

PAGE 6.

Hour, Date, Place	Summary of Events and Information	Remarks and references to Appendices
Oct 20 (cont)	117th Bty reported that the enemy had completed an intermediate trench between SNAG & GIRD LINE. The Bty was heavily shelled. 116th Registration only.	
21.	20th Bty registration only. 0800 116th Bty. 117th Bty fired on S.O.S. line at 5.30 pm. 8.0 pm heavy shelling changed the day. 51st Bde R.F.A. relieved 53rd Bde R.F.A. (the 117th were not informed until the relief had been effected) operation orders for attack on GIRD LINE received.	
22.	20th Bty registered fired on GIRD LINE for barrage. 116th registration only. 117th had bursts for attack M17 & 7 1/2. 730x on extensive syst. 680 rounds fired in order to demolish the portion of the trench. The line was charged later. S.O.S at 8.30 p.m.	
23.	40th Bty attempted unsuccessfully to register with an aeroplane (not ready). 117th Bty had a quiet day.	1 O.R. wounded 117 Bty

WAR DIARY
or
INTELLIGENCE SUMMARY.
(Erase heading not required.)

Army Form C. 2118.

PAGE 7

Hour, Date, Place	Summary of Events and Information	Remarks and references to Appendices
Oct 23(a)	116th Bty fired a short preliminary bombardment and left in support of an attack on TAIL TRENCH by the 9th Division, the attack was unsuccessful.	
24	Every misty weather, 40th Bty nothing to report. 116th Bty registered GIRD LINE and QUARRIES. 50th Division relieved 9th Division in the trenches. 111th Bty a slow bombardment of GIRDLINE was carried out and the new trenches to front of it.	
	Regtl. firing for four hours by 116th Bty various operations were carried out and observed during a fine period from Oct. 24 to 31st.	
25.	40th fired with success on the GIRD LINE (500 rds) 111th carried out slow bombardment of GIRD on also did the 116th Bty, who on a double fired for four hours during the night.	2/Lieut. R.E. GOULD posted to 111th from D.A.C.

WAR DIARY or INTELLIGENCE SUMMARY

Army Form C. 2118.

PAGE 8.

(Erase heading not required.)

Hour, Date, Place	Summary of Events and Information	Remarks and references to Appendices
Oct 26	4.0ᵈ re-registered GIRD LINE & BLIND TRENCH and at 4.0 pm fired a party of Germans seen to leave a trench which was heavily shelled. our howrs. 116 & 117 carried out bombardment of GIRD LINE during the day. 116ᵉ four hours night firing. At 7 pm SOS fired by 117ᵉ Bty. for 5 minutes.	
27.	20ᵉ fired on SOS for short time to answer to infantry flares. 117ᵉ fired lines on SOS between 4.30 pm & 4.50 pm. Slow rate of one GIRD LINE by 116ᵉ & 117ᵉ Bty. 116ᵉ fired during the night.	
28.	4.0ᵈ Bty. re-registered GIRD LINE also COUPE GEURE TRENCH. fired on parties in LE BARQUE road. 116 & 117. Quiet day. night firing by 116ᵉ Bty.	

WAR DIARY
or
INTELLIGENCE SUMMARY.
(Erase heading not required.)

Army Form C. 2118.

PAGE 9

Hour, Date, Place	Summary of Events and Information	Remarks and references to Appendices
Oct 29th	Quiet day for all batteries.	
30.	40" fired 100 rounds per hour from midnight till dawn searching for roads beyond BIRD LINE	2 O.R. wounded 11pm
	117" registered BIRD LINE intermediate trench	
	M4 fired on BIRD LINE	
31.	40" Bty, re grenades fired gun shells at 12.30am + 4.0 am on BIRD LINE. 116 + 117 Quiet day.	

G.B.Mimms
Lt. Col. R.G.A.
O/C 26th Bde R.G.A.

1st Divisional Artillery.

H. Q. 26th BRIGADE R.F.A. ::: NOVEMBER 1916.

NOVEMBER 1916

WAR DIARY
or
INTELLIGENCE SUMMARY 4th Bde R.F.A

Army Form C. 2118.

PAGE 1.

Hour, Date, Place	Summary of Events and Information	Remarks and references to Appendices
BEHENCOURT 1 Ref. Sheet 62^D 1st Edition 1/40.000 6.19.a.	The Batteries of the Brigade were in action as follows: – The 40th (how) Bty attached to 39th Bde R.F.A., the 16th Battery attached to 75th Bde R.F.A., the 117th Bty attached to 53rd Bde R.F.A. With regard to the 117th Bty R.F.A. – the log-book of this battery was destroyed by shell fire and the period from Nov 1st to 18th cannot therefore be recorded with accuracy of detail, during this said period the battery bombarded at intervals by day & night the GIRD LINE and vicinity in N.11 & 17 & trenches round and about the BUTTE DE WARLENCOURT and also took part in an attack by the 50th Division on the GIRD LINE. The Battery pulled out of action on the 18th inst. 40th Bty fired 50 rounds gas shell behind GIVOLINE	The 117th Bty were in action at M.36.a.2.1 Ref map 57c S.W. 1/20.000 in an exposed position where they were heavily shelled consistently. The 16th Bty in action about S.3.C.8.5. The 40th Bty in action at M.33.a.1.6. Ref map 57c D.1.5.1/2. Ref 57c S.W. 1/20.000

PAGE 2

Army Form C. 2118.

WAR DIARY
or
INTELLIGENCE SUMMARY.
(Erase heading not required.)

Instructions regarding War Diaries and Intelligence Summaries are contained in F.S. Regs., Part II. and the Staff Manual respectively. Title pages will be prepared in manuscript.

Hour, Date, Place	Summary of Events and Information	Remarks and references to Appendices
1 (contd)	At 7 p.m. 116th in Registration in preparation for an attack by 50th Division on Z. day	
2.	Registration only	
3.	40th engaged enemy transport N. of Spitaten 40th shelled GIRO LINE at 9.0 a.m & 1.15 p.m.	
4.	116 fired a lot of barrages conjunction with other batteries of 25th Bde at 9 a.m & 1.15 p.m	
5.	Attack on GIRD LINE & BUTTE DE WARLENCOURT by the brigade of 50th Division at 9.10 a.m. 2 co. 40. 116. & 117 OS(?) all fired in support of this attack which appeared to be successful except on the right by BAPAUME road (?) however our infantry were reported to be back in our own front line in the evening. A creeping barrage was fired by batteries the three barrage being COUPE LINE & the volumes and unknown	

WAR DIARY
or
INTELLIGENCE SUMMARY.
(Erase heading not required.)

PAGE 3.

Army Form C. 2118.

Hour, Date, Place	Summary of Events and Information	Remarks and references to Appendices
5 contd.	Late in the afternoon, during this time the 90th constantly engaged enemy's infantry in the open in M.5.c. N.1.a. enemy made two attempts to advance but was checked each time by artillery fire.	
6/9	the Chiery of pieces to fire.	
10.	90" engaged enemy transport on road in N.1.a. S.O.S. at 10 p.m.	
11.	90" had S.O.S. east at 1.30 a.m. and at 12-3 p.m. took part in a CHINESE ATTACK on GIRO LINE. 116" Battery took part in the preparation of an attack by 50th Division on GIRO LINE been HOOK SAP attack was partially successful but infantry returned their trenches the following day.	

WAR DIARY or INTELLIGENCE SUMMARY

PAGE 4.

Army Form C. 2118.

Hour, Date, Place	Summary of Events and Information	Remarks and references to Appendices
12.	40th engaged a party of 300 Germans in the open ast in M6a dispersed this party & inflicting casualties.	
13.	A Chinese attack took place at 5.45am in co-operation with an attack by the 5th Army, if available battery took part in the Chinese attack.	
14.	The 50th Division + ANZAC CORPS on the GIRD LINE, the 40th Bty fired in support of this and also on Germans seen in the open in N1a. The Bty were shelled during the day.	
15.	Nothing of interest.	
16.	40 Bty fired on GIRD LINE + HOOK SAP.	
17.	116th took part in a Chinese attack at 6.10 am	

WAR DIARY PAGE 5
or
INTELLIGENCE SUMMARY

Army Form C. 2118.

(Erase heading not required.)

Hour, Date, Place	Summary of Events and Information	Remarks and references to Appendices
18.	40th fired 130 rounds on S.O.S. LINE between 10.0 a.m. & noon, received S.O.S. at 4 p.m. The 1st Inf. Bde 1st Division commenced to relieve the 50th Division infantry	
19/20.	Nothing of interest to report.	
BOTTOM WOOD 21. Sheet 57cSW 1/40,000	40th bombarded the BUTTE DE WARLENCOURT	
22/23/24.	Alsenehia river, for 20 minutes. HQ moved up to BOTTOM WOOD. Bad weather, nothing of importance from the 40th Bty the 116th Bty became responsible for a new zone M18c A.7 to M18c O.9.	
S15c.6.2. Sheet 57cS.W. 1/40,000	25. 40th fired 100 rounds on HOOK SAP. 116th registration H.Q. took over from 35th Bde H.Q. at S15c.6.2. and the responsibility for the defence of "C" sector. N18a O.O. & M 15c central.	Sheet 57cSW 1/40000
	26. Quiet day & observation bad.	

Army Form C. 2118.

WAR DIARY
or
INTELLIGENCE SUMMARY.
(Erase heading not required.)

PAGE 6.

Instructions regarding War Diaries and Intelligence Summaries are contained in F.S. Regs., Part II. and the Staff Manual respectively. Title pages will be prepared in manuscript.

Hour, Date, Place	Summary of Events and Information	Remarks and references to Appendices
27.	Enemy artillery fairly active, FAUCOURT L'ABBAYE was bombarded heavily, bad observation.	Sheet 57cSh 1/20.000
28.	Very quiet day.	
29.	Heavy mist rendered observation impossible. 40" shelled GIRDLINE Posts.	
30.	EAUCOURT L'ABBAYE again shelled otherwise quiet day.	
	NOTE. During the whole of this month the 15th Battery are at the 4.5 How. pit, for I have and kept in the roads that behind the enemy lines, in conjunction with other batteries in the group.	
	Ref: map for trenches LIGNY-THILLOY.	1/20.000

C.R.Simkin
Lt. Col. RA.
Cmmt 36 Bde RFA.

WAR DIARY
or
INTELLIGENCE SUMMARY.
(Erase heading not required.)

Army Form C. 2118.

Hour, Date, Place	Summary of Events and Information	Remarks and references to Appendices
	Casualties Portugal November 1916.	
1.	Lt. G.F. Samuels posted to Heavy Bt.	
	19 Corps.	
3.	2 O.R. 117 killed 1 O.R. 117 wounded 1 O.R. 40 wounded.	
5.	1 O.R. 40 wounded.	
14.	1 O.R. H.Q. wounded.	

1st Divisional Artillery.

H. Q. 26th BRIGADE R.F.A. ::: DECEMBER 1916.

Army Form C. 2118.

WAR DIARY
or
INTELLIGENCE SUMMARY.

(Erase heading not required.)

76th Brigade R.F.A.
1st Division, III Corps, 4th Army.

Place	Date	Hour	Summary of Events and Information during DECEMBER 1916.	Remarks and references to Appendices
S.15.c.6.1.	1.1.		As stated last month the H.Q. 76 Bde R.F.A. took over from 75th Bde. the responsibility for the defence of "C" sector - M18a O.O. to M18c centre.	Ref. Corps Siege maps
Nr. BAZENTIN			Most day enemy's system and approaches were bombarded	LIGNY-THILLOY 1/20,000
LE GRAND	2		Shelling as usual of FAUCOURT L'ABBAYE	
Map Sheet	3		Enemy more active than usual on our trenches.	
57c S.W.	4		Normal day	
Edn. 3 D 2,500	5		Artillery activity about rather than normal.	
	6		The Divisional front was re-arranged and the Infantry relief in connection with this having been completed on the night 5/6th the Divisional front is now divided into three Groups as follows: Right Group, 2nd Inf. Bde in the line, from a line through N.14a.O.O. - N.19.b.77 to a line N.13.c.O.O. - LIGNY-THILLOY CHURCH (N.7.b.53.4.) CENTRE GROUP 3rd Inf. Bde in the line, from a line N.13.c.O.O. - LIGNY-THILLOY CHURCH to a North South line through N.7.a.4.8. LEFT GROUP 1st Inf. Bde in the line, from a North South line through N.7.a.4.8. to a line through M.11.a.6.3. - M.17a.R.O. ¶ O/C 76 Bde was responsible for the defence of the CENTRE GROUP front.	

Army Form C. 2118.

WAR DIARY
or
INTELLIGENCE SUMMARY.
(Erase heading not required.)

Instructions regarding War Diaries and Intelligence Summaries are contained in F. S. Regs., Part II. and the Staff Manual respectively. Title pages will be prepared in manuscript.

Place	Date	Hour	Summary of Events and Information	Remarks and references to Appendices
	7/5		Normal	
	9		" B/3S1 Bde R.F.A relieved B/3S2 Bde R.F.A and came under orders of Bertie Group.	
	10-14		Normal day. A+C/3SD relieved A+B/3S2 and came under Bertie Group on 14th	
	15		At 7 a.m Bertie Group co-operated with trench mortars making German and intense bombardment of the MAZE (German salient in M 24 a & b) for ten minutes.	
	16		Quiet day.	
	17		Very quiet day. One section of 40th Bty relieved by section of 30th Bty	
	18		Relief of 40th Bty completed. 30² Bty came under orders of Bertie Group. 40" under O.C. 39" Bde R.F.A marched to billets at MOLLIENS-AU-BOIS.	
	19		Enemy have active in own trenches. Normal	
	20		Normal	
	21		Normal	
	22/24		Normal	

T2134. Wt W708—776. 500000. 4/15. Sir J. C. & S.

WAR DIARY
or
INTELLIGENCE SUMMARY
(Erase heading not required.)

Army Form C. 2118.

Place	Date	Hour	Summary of Events and Information	Remarks and references to Appendices
	25		Slightly increased activity on both sides.	
	26		Great aeroplane activity. The 116 Battery position was shelled during the evening from casualties. damaging one gun slightly and exploding about 100 rds of ammunition. Bombardment of enemy system from 6am to 4pm in conjunction with the Heavies.	K.13.c.
	27		Enemy strong points were shelled during the day.	
	28		Bombardment from 8am to 4pm of the MAZE (German salient in M24.d) at 6.5pm. made by 2nd Roy Munster Fusiliers in liaison against the MAZE, in which trench mortars co-operated, discovered the trenches to be almost obliterated & empty.	
	29		Quiet day. The section of 116 Bty relieved by B/250 Bde R.F.A. the relieved section marched to billets at MOULLENS-AU-BOIS.	
	30		Enemy were active on our front again in am. Relief of 116 Bty completed.	
	31		116 Bty marched to billets at MOLLIENS-AU-BOIS. B/120 Bde R.F.A came under orders of Cercle Group. Relief of Eleven Infantry bt Eleven Infantry in progress.	

Army Form C. 2118.

WAR DIARY
or
INTELLIGENCE SUMMARY.
(Erase heading not required.)

Instructions regarding War Diaries and Intelligence Summaries are contained in F. S. Regs., Part II. and the Staff Manual respectively. Title pages will be prepared in manuscript.

Place	Date	Hour	Summary of Events and Information	Remarks and references to Appendices
	31.		Normal day. Relief of 1st Division by 50th Division completed.	
			Casualties Postings December 1916.	
	14		1 O.R. wounded 116 Bty.	
	16		2 O.R. killed 3 O.R. wounded 116 Bty.	
	22		2/Lieut R.C. Knowles struck off the strength of 117 Bty. Medical board in England H.Q. (A.G. La Noted 22.12.16.	
	2.		2/Lieut R.E. Lowcol invalided to England 2/12/16.	
	13		2/Lieut H.B. Ince to 117 Bty. from D.A.C.	
	1-1-17.			

J.H. Tantoumshayn to Lt Col. R.D.A.
Cmg 76 Bde R.D.A.

1ST DIVISION
ROYAL ARTILLERY

26TH BRIGADE, R.F.A.
JAN - MAR 1917

WAR DIARY.

26th. Brigade, Royal Field Artillery.

1st. DIVISION.

January. 1917.

JANUARY 1917

WAR DIARY
or
INTELLIGENCE SUMMARY

76 Brigade R.F.A.

Place	Date	Hour	Summary of Events and Information	Remarks and references to Appendices
S.15.c.6.1. Map = 57c S.W. Edtn. 2.D.	1.		Normal day. Right of 31st Dec/1st of January/17.	
	2/3		Remainder of 116th Bty R.F.A. relieved by B/250 Bde R.F.A. and marched to billet at MOLLIENS-AU-BOIS. Normal days.	Ref 162 D. M.G. B/S
	4.		Head Quarters were relieved by H.Q. 250th Bde R.F.A. and proceeded to wagon lines in S.26.A. (Sheet 57c S.W. Edtn. 2D).	
	5/6		At wagon lines H.Q., 116th & 40th Bty at MOLLIENS-AU-BOIS (refatrve), 117th Bty in action.	
	7.		117th Bty commenced to hand over to 54th Bty R.M. on section only, which proceeded to MOLLIENS-AU-BOIS, as did also Head Quarters.	
	8.		Relief of 117th Bty by 54th Bty completed, remainder of 117th Bty marched to MOLLIENS-AU-BOIS.	
MOLLIENS AU BOIS.	9/14		At rest. On the 14th inst the scheme of re-organisation came to force. The 40th (How) Bty left the 76th Bde R.M. 33rd Division joined the 25th Bde and A/Bty of 116 Bde R.M. 33rd Division joined the 76th Bde as H/76 Bty. The 76th Bde R.F.A. became an Army Field Artillery Bde but was attached to 1st Division for administration	

Place	Date	Hour	Summary of Events and Information	Remarks and references to Appendices
MOLLIENS AU BOIS	1/6 a.a		No 1 section of 1st D.A.C. less the howitzer portion plus a portion of the 23rd D.A.C. became the 76th Brigade Ammunition Column.	
	15/28		As read.	
	29th		The Brigade marched from MOLLIENS AU BOIS to VILLERS BRETONNEUX. Pg/62 D. this step preparatory to taking over a part of the line from the French troops.	
	30/31		Resting at VILLERS BRETONNEUX.	
			Casualties ~ Postings.	
			Casualties NIL.	
			Postings.	
	a		2/Lieut G.A. PEUCHEN from 1st D.A.C. to H.Q. 76 Bde R.M.	
	14		B/76. BSM. Major H.D. LITTLEJOHN (to hospital) B.A.C. from 1st D.A.C. 14/1/17	
			2/Lt. L.G. GARY ELMES, 2/Lt. N. HEWITT {Major W. THOMPSON, 2/Lt. J.H.W. CUDMORE	
			" C.W. WEEKES " F. ATHERTON	
			Capt. K.J. SNOWDEN (27.1.17) T.A. WARD. G. Shinnin Lt Col R.A.	
	14		2/Lts R.T. DAVIDSON, H.S. BEALE (BAC.) O.C. 76 Bde R.F.A.	

WAR DIARY.

26th. Brigade, Royal Field Artillery.

1st. DIVISION.

February. 1917.

Army Form C. 2118.

WAR DIARY
or
INTELLIGENCE SUMMARY
(Erase heading not required.)

FEBRUARY 1917

26th Brigade R.F.A.

Place	Date	Hour	Summary of Events and Information	Remarks and references to Appendices
VILLERS BRETTONNEUX	1/6		At rest.	Ref. 62 2/100000
	7		The Brigade less A/26 Btty. marched from VILLERS BRETTONEUX to wagon lines in wood R.5.b & R.6.a previously to relieving the FRENCH. Night of 7/8 one section of 116th Btty relieved one section of 6th Btty. A.D.24 at N7.c.7½.8½ and one section of 117th Btty relieved one section of 2nd Btty. A.D.24. at N2.b.1.5.	Ref 62 S.W. EDT N.2
	8		Night 8/9 116th Btty. Completed relief, one section relieving remaining section of 6th Btty AD 24 and one section relieving one section of 5th Btty. A.D.24. 117th Btty. Completed relief, one section relieving remaining section of 2nd Btty. and one relieving one section of 3rd Btty, A.D.24	
	9		Head Quarters moved from wagon line to M.6.d.5½ to relieve Head Quarters of 2nd Group AD 24.	
M6d5½ map=Sheet 62c SW EDT 2	10		Relief of FRENCH completed. The Division covers the front from N.2.d.73 to N.12.b.76. This is covered by Left Group (N.12.b.76 to N.17 central) and Right Group (N.17 central to N.12.b.76). The	

WAR DIARY
or
INTELLIGENCE SUMMARY.

Army Form C. 2118.

PAGE 2

Place	Date	Hour	Summary of Events and Information	Remarks and references to Appendices
N6 d 5 1/2 Map = Sheet 62 C.S.W ED.2A	10		Right Group is commanded by H.Q 26th Bde. R.F.A and consists of 113th, 114th, 115th, 116 & 40th How. The 117th Btty is in the left group which is commanded by 39 Q 39th Bde R.F.A. The 48th Division hold the line on our left and the FRENCH on our right	
	11		Night 11/12 Division front becomes N12 a 81 to N29 a 23. The Right group handing over all front north of N17 c 43 to left group and taking over as far south as N29 a 21 from 35th Divisional Artillery (FRENCH)	Ref 62 C sw 1/20,000
	12		Normal Day	
	13		A/26 Btty moved from VILLERS BRETTONNEUX to VAIRE. Night of 13/14 extended the Right group front as far south as N29 Ref 62 C SW C.14 (VILLERS-CARBONNEL ESTREE ROAD) Taking over from the FRENCH	Ref 62 D K 1/40,000 Ref 62 C SW 1/20,000
14/2 1			Normal Day	
	22		A/26 Btty moved from VAIRE to wagon lines L 28 c 91	Ref 62 D K 1/40,000
	23		At 7.30 P.M the 149th Bde, 50th Division who are on our immediate	

WAR DIARY
INTELLIGENCE SUMMARY.

Place	Date	Hour	Summary of Events and Information	Remarks and references to Appendices
M6 d 5-1½ map = sheet 62c SW Ed 2A	23		right, thinking they were going to be attacked fired an S.O.S. The Right group bright O P sent an SOS out claiming to have seen an SOS signal go up on our right front. I have says were repeated. The two S.O.S were fired. The Right Battalion claim not to have sent up the SOS signal.	
	24		Normal Day	
	25		night of 25/26, one section of A/26 Btty went into action at H34 b-79 under 48 the D.A. Left Sub Group.	Ref 62 c/40000
	26/25		Normal Days	
			Casualties & Postings Casualties	
			3 Major H A LITTLETHON (struck off the strength)	
			20 2/Lt F. ATHERTON (struck off the strength) } sick	
			24 2/Lt. E A RYRIE (struck off the strength)	
			Postings nil	

G. S. Kirin M Lt. Col R F A
C at 26th Bde R F A

WAR DIARY.

26th. Brigade, Royal Field Artillery.

1st. DIVISION.

MARCH. 1917.

Army A Fr. April
J B Z

26th Brigade R.F.A.

MARCH 1917

PAGE 1.

Army Form C. 2118.

WAR DIARY
or
INTELLIGENCE SUMMARY.
(Erase heading not required.)

Place	Date	Hour	Summary of Events and Information	Remarks and references to Appendices
Ref Sheet 1 62 SW M6d 5½ 2	1		Hostile aeroplanes and artillery more active than usual	
	2		Normal day.	
	3		Night of 3/4 one section of 114th Btty. comes out of action and proceeds to wagon lines en route for 5th Army school	
	4		Normal day	
	5		Head Quarters of 26th Bde relieved by 316 & 120th Bde night of 5/6. Bde proceed to wagon lines. and A/26 Batteries come out of action and proceed to wagon lines.	
Rottenell	6		The Brigade marched from wagon lines to FOUILLOY. The 26th B.A.C. joining the Brigade en route at MERICOURT of 62 Divsn	
	7		The Brigade marched to VILLERS-BOCAGE	
VILLERS-BOCAGE	8		The Brigade marched to OUTRE BOIS (D4)	
OUTREBOIS	9		The Brigade marched to FALAMETZ (B3). The 115th Btty	

WAR DIARY or INTELLIGENCE SUMMARY.

Army Form C. 2118. PAGE 2.

Place	Date	Hour	Summary of Events and Information	Remarks and references to Appendices
Ref. Lens II 1/100,000 BUTHEBUS FILLIÈVRES	9. 10.		and B.A.C. billeting at FILLIÈVRES (B3) The Brigade marched from GALAMETZ to BERGUENEUF -SÉ (D1). The 117th and A/26 Bttys and B.A.C. billeting at ANVIN (D1)	Ref. Lens II 1/100,000
BERGUENEUF HOUDAIN ESTRÉE-CAUCHIE	11. 12. 13/19 20.		The Brigade marched to HOUDAIN (G.1) the Brigade marched to ESTREE-CAUCHIE (H.2) at rest. The 26th B.A.C. marched to ECOIVRES. The 26 Bde less B.A.C. march to wagon lines (F.7d) night 21/22 half batteries go into action the Bty at ROLINCOURT positions. 116th Bty at A.20.a.63½ (B.3) RT.51 NW A.20.a.44 (B.2). A/26 Bty at A.20.a.53 (B.1). The 26 Bde HQ go into action at A.25.b.½.7 (B HQ) under the command of H.Q. Right group of 1st C.D.A. night of 22 nof 23 not the remaining half batteries of 116, 117 and A/26 Bttys go into action	Ref 51 N.E. F.7.2
Ref 51NE 2 F.7d				

WAR DIARY
or
INTELLIGENCE SUMMARY.

Place	Date	Hour	Summary of Events and Information	Remarks and references to Appendices
of 51 NE D2. F7d	22		The Bde is in action as a silent Bde for the purpose of building a forward position and bringing up ammunition.	
ROLINCOURT 13 NW1 E D5 25.b.27.25	23/24		Work on forward positions carried out and ammunition brought up. Batteries shelled one 9.4" heavy bright 16 of 26th Bde R.F.A. night 25.b.26.B position when out of action 5.b.26 Bde HQ moving to wagon lines. 7.b.26 Bde batteries moving to positions. The 116th Btty at A 21 c 63½ ROLINCOURT (1). The 117th Btty at A 21 a 75 7½ (L2). The A/26 Btty at 57 NW1 E D5 at A 15 c 8½ 2 (L3)	
at 57 N E 26/31 D2 F7d	26/31		Batteries positions improved and ammunition brought up. Registration carried under cover of firing of other batteries.	

PAGE 4.

Casualties and Postings

Casualties
2/Lt D.G. CARY ELWES (Hospital sick) 29/3/17

Postings
Major H.N. FAIRBANK to 30 D.A. 18/3/17
2/Lt W.A. SEARLE from 22nd Bde R.F.A. to A/26 Btty 24/3/17

G.H.Winton
Lt. Col. R.F.A.
Comdg. 26th Bde. R.F.A.

www.ingramcontent.com/pod-product-compliance
Lightning Source LLC
Chambersburg PA
CBHW080905230426
43664CB00016B/2729